HARNEY, "DAT'S LOVE"

Eileen Darby — Graphic House

Carmen Jones

BY

OSCAR HAMMERSTEIN II

BASED ON

MEILHAC AND HALÉVY'S ADAPTATION OF

PROSPER MERIMÉE'S

CARMEN

1945

ALFRED A KNOPF

This play is not at present released for the use of non-professional groups. When it is released, the non-professional rights will be controlled exclusively by Dorothy B. Hammerstein, 11 East 44th Street, New York 17, N. Y. without whose permission in writing no performance may be given.

Manufactured in the United States of America

FIRST EDITION

To
DOROTHY

*B*elieving CARMEN to be a perfect wedding of story and music, we have adhered, as closely as possible, to its original form. All the melodies — with a few very minor exceptions — are sung in their accustomed order. The small deviations we have made were only those which seemed honestly demanded by a transference of CARMEN to a modern American background.

In our elimination of the recitative passages, we are not taking as great a liberty as may be supposed. Bizet and his collaborators originally wrote CARMEN with spoken dialogue scenes between the airs that were sung. The work was intended for theatres of average size, like the Opéra Comique in Paris (where it is played today as a dialogue opera).

CARMEN was not converted to a "grand opera" until after Bizet's death. The music set to the dialogue is not his music. It was written by Ernest Guiraud.

OSCAR HAMMERSTEIN II

The *BROADWAY THEATRE*

NEW YORK CITY

Beginning T HURSDAY, December 2, 1943

BILLY ROSE

PRESENTS

Carmen Jones

BY

OSCAR HAMMERSTEIN II

BASED ON

MEILHAC AND HALÉVY'S ADAPTATION OF
PROSPER MERIMÉE'S

CARMEN

MUSIC BY

GEORGES BIZET

Staging, lighting, and color schemes
of entire production by

HASSARD SHORT

Libretto directed by CHARLES FRIEDMAN
New orchestral arrangements by
ROBERT RUSSELL BENNETT
Settings designed by HOWARD BAY
Costumes designed by RAOUL PÈNE DUBOIS
Choreography by EUGENE LORING
Choral direction by ROBERT SHAW
Orchestra conducted by JOSEPH LITTAU

Cast

CORPORAL MORREL	Napoleon Reed *or* Robert Clarke
FOREMAN	Robert Clarke *or* George Willis
CINDY LOU	Carlotta Franzell *or* Elton J. Warren
SERGEANT BROWN	Jack Carr
JOE	Luther Saxon *or* Napoleon Reed
CARMEN	Muriel Smith *or* Muriel Rahn
SALLY	Sibol Cain
T-BONE	Edward Roche
TOUGH KID	William Jones
DRUMMER	Cosy Cole
BARTENDER	Melvin Howard
WAITER	Edward Christopher
FRANKIE	June Hawkins
MYRT	Jessica Russell
RUM	Edward Lee Tyler
DINK	Dick Montgomery
HUSKY MILLER	Glenn Bryant
BOY	J. Flashe Riley
GIRL	Royce Wallace
SOLDIERS	Robert Clarke William Woolfolk George Willis Elijah Hodges
MR. HIGGINS	P. Jay Sidney
MISS HIGGINS	Fredye Marshall
PHOTOGRAPHER	Alford Pierre

CARD PLAYERS	⎧ Urylee Leonardos ⎨ Ethel White ⎩ Sibol Cain
DANCING GIRL	Ruth Crumpton
PONCHO	William Dillard
DANCING BOXERS	⎧ Sheldon B. Hoskins ⎩ Randolph Sawyer
BULLET HEAD	Melvin Howard
REFEREE	Tony Fleming, Jr.

SOLDIERS, FACTORY WORKERS, SOCIALITES

Synopsis of Scenes

Musical Sequence

x

Musical Sequence

Introduction

WHEN I WAS a small boy, "opera" was a bad word in our home. Opera was a way people lost money, especially Grandpa. Grandpa was a clever man. He was a publisher, an inventor, a builder of theatres, and a theatrical producer. Whenever he was engaged in any of these pursuits our family was rich. As soon as he would get enough money together he would put it all into opera and the family would become poor again.

I began to be curious about this word. My father and Uncle Arthur couldn't mention it without using swear words in the same sentence. What was it? "It's like a show," Mother said, "only the actors sing all their lines instead of speaking them." This sounded pretty silly to me, but the more I thought it over, the more I wanted to see these strange goings-on. Warned that opera was "too heavy" for children, I nevertheless persisted until I was taken to a matinee at the Manhattan Opera House.

Well! My mother hadn't told me the worst. Not only were they singing everything, but everything was in a language I couldn't understand! "What are they singing?" I whispered to Mother. "Italian." I looked around at the audience. "Do all these people know Italian?" "Only a few," she answered. "Then why do they sing it in Italian, Mother?" "They always do. Stop asking questions."

No wonder she told me to stop asking questions. There is no sensible answer to that one and she knew

it. I sat back in the well-cushioned orchestra chair —
Grandpa built beautiful opera houses — and I found
myself enjoying the lovely music coming up from the
orchestra pit. But I was puzzled and disturbed by the
accompanying action on the stage. Sometimes the fat
lady would look very sad, and there was no way of
knowing why. Sometimes she laughed, but I wouldn't
know what the joke was and I wished I did. It then
seemed quite clear to me why Grandpa lost money
on opera. Listening to people sing words you didn't
understand wasn't much fun. That's what I thought
then. That's what I think now.

There is no mystery why the people of Europe enjoy and support opera and the people of the United
States do not. When an opera of German or Italian
origin is sung in Paris, the public hear it in their own
language, French. The Germans and Italians are also
provided with this elementary advantage of hearing
operas translated into their own language. They
wouldn't like it any more than Americans do if the
story was a secret shared by the cast and the conductor.
They too would feel out of things, just as we do. And
they'd stay away from opera houses, as we do. There
is a strange theory in this country that opera is "over
our heads." It isn't at all. It just by-passes us and re-
fuses to communicate with us. If you're not a linguist,
you're just out of luck.

To the plea for opera in English there is a stock
answer. "It has always failed." This happens to be
true, and it seems like pretty crushing evidence against
our side. But there's a joker hidden in this answer. The
sad fact is that when you hear opera in English it is

in pretty bad English. These great works, originally written by distinguished dramatic poets, are translated by scholarly but untalented gentlemen who know nearly nothing about the science of writing phonetic, singable lyrics. They are not poets, nor dramatists, nor showmen. A good adaptation of an opera requires a librettist who is all of these.

Thus, when opera in English has failed, it is the translations that have been rejected, and rightly so. The public has not rejected "opera in English," because it has never had a skillful English version of an opera submitted to it.

I feel in my bloodstream the approach of that choleric indignation that invariably seizes me when I discuss this topic. I am beginning to sweat, and this is not a hot day. I must control myself, else I will be taking wild swipes at my list of very special hates: the dear singing teachers who instruct their pupils to broaden every "a" so that a lovely word like "romance" becomes "romonce" — no word at all; the foreign singer whose accent makes English less intelligible than his own tongue; the conductor who thinks there is more entertainment in a blast from a horn than in any English word that could possibly be sung. But I must forbear. This is not the day for me to handle these opera-house barnacles as they should be handled. I am, in fact, supposed to be writing an introduction to *Carmen Jones*. And all that I have said so far bears only indirect relevance to my assigned subject. For *Carmen Jones* is not the answer to your prayers or mine for opera in English. *Carmen Jones* is not even an opera. It is a musical play, based on an opera. *Car-*

men Jones, however, does prove this much: that a sur-
prisingly large number of the regular theatre-going
public will enjoy operatic music if you let them in on
the story. However unconventional may be my treat-
ment of the original work, the score remains an operatic score, and the story, in its spirt and rendition,
is an operatic story. It is a tragedy. Yet it has appealed
to the same public that nightly patronizes musical
comedy.

The most interesting indication that opera is not
"over the heads of the theatrical public" is the last
scene of *Carmen Jones.* After being given a noisy
greeting by his admirers, Husky Miller is marched off
into the stadium, and the scene thins down to just Carmen and Joe. He makes the last desperate effort to
get her to come back to him. For twelve minutes they
sing — not *Hit Parade* melodies, verses and choruses,
but sincere musical expressions of their emotions, just
as do Carmen and Don José in the original work.
Throughout this distinctly "operatic" sequence, the
audience is held as at no other time in the evening.
They are tense and still in their seats. There is no
doubt that they are interested and there is no doubt
that this is opera. In one respect it is better-than-usual
opera, because the characters look their parts. And
they are acting as well as singing. They are not waving
their arms and pounding the stage like heavy-footed
mastodons. They are not using that phony sob-in-the-
throat trick of grand-opera singers in emotional passages. They are portraying two human beings in ter-
rible trouble, two confused souls moving towards their
destruction with every word they sing. The audience,

knowing what the words mean, are held in a tight grip of interest until the tragedy finds its inevitable end and Carmen sinks to the floor, stabbed by her crazed, heart-torn lover.

Carmen Jones is an indication, if not positive proof, that opera in English may be popular if the lyrics are singable, understandable, and dramatic. A more complete proof would be an adaptation of the original, keeping the scene in Spain and all details the same except for the exigencies of translation. Some day someone who understands music and the theatre will write a straight English version of some opera, and some courageous director will force the singers to act in a sensible manner — and the result will be astounding!

Carmen Jones, however, does not blaze this trail. *Carmen Jones* is designed to play eight performances a week, for as many weeks as the public will come. It is designed for the same theatres that play musical comedies. Therefore there is not room for ninety men in the orchestra pit. We use thirty-three. Our chorus is not so large as a grand-opera chorus. We have moments of dancing integrated into the performance throughout the evening. It is lavishly produced by Billy Rose, and in a modern manner. It is not grand opera.

The musical play *Carmen Jones* is, nevertheless, a very direct descendant of the opera *Carmen*. Bizet's score has not been reorchestrated, nor have the traditional tempi been altered. The arias are sung in their original order and in their proper places in the unfolding of the plot. Two melodies were cut. A few repeated passages have been cut. The recitative has been supplanted by dialogue. This last liberty is, indeed, no liberty at all, for the very first version, as produced at the Opéra Comique in Paris in 1875, used dialogue in these very spots. The recitatives were written in later, and not by Bizet, but by Guiraud.

I want to establish that my choice of Negroes as the principal figures in the story was not motivated by any desire to pull an eccentric theatrical stunt. It is a logical result of my decision to write a modern American version of *Carmen*. The nearest thing in our modern American life to an equivalent of the gypsies in Spain is the Negro. Like the gypsy, he expresses his feelings simply, honestly, and graphically. Also as with the gypsy there is rhythm in his body, and music in his heart. The score of *Carmen* is a Frenchman's version of Spanish music. Do not forget, however, that Spanish music was deeply influenced by the Moors from Africa. The rhythm of the "Habanera" is even closer to the home of Carmen Jones. It is a West Indian rhythm exported to Spain, heard and imitated by Bizet. I mention these academic facts without being very much impressed by them myself. My belief about words and music is that when a melody is good to hear, it can take on any color the lyric gives it. My favorite example is a song by Irving Berlin called "Blue Skies." It is a bright, optimistic lyric, as the title suggests. Hum the melody slowly, without the happy words and you will immediatley realize that it has the quality of an Oriental lament!

So much for the flexibility of music. Now, when it comes to story, any truly great story is equally great no matter where you set it or in what period you play

Introduction

it. This is because the motives are honest and not forced. If the events in the plot are a natural outgrowth of what the characters would do to one another in real life, they will stand the test of any transplanting.

Many people who love opera have expressed their pleasure with *Carmen Jones*. Others with more reverence in their affection have been shocked and offended by it. If in the eyes of these latter I have desecrated a masterpiece, I can only say to them: "I am sorry. I didn't mean to." I share their affection and reverence for *Carmen*. Prosper Merimée's romance is one of the world's ageless tales. Meilhac and Halévy's libretto is a model of musical-drama architecture. I learned a great deal from my study of their work. Bizet's score is the best musical expression of a story that I know of. Setting words to it was an exciting experience. I have too deep and real a respect for this fine opera willfully to hurt it. If there has been desecration, charge it not to literary vandalism but to my bad taste and ignorance. Within the limits of my taste and knowledge I sincerely believe *Carmen Jones* to be an effective and interesting musical play. I am glad I wrote it.

Cast

Corporal Morrel
Cindy Lou
Joe
Sergeant Brown
Carmen Jones
Myrt ⎫
Frankie ⎭ *Her girl friends*
Husky Miller
Rum *Husky Miller's Manager*
Dink *Rum's henchman*

SMALLER PARTS

Foreman
Sally
T-Bone
Tough Kid
The President *of the Meadow Lawn Country Club*
Bartender
A Photographer
Miss Higgins
Poncho the Panther *Husky's opponent*
Bullet Head *Husky's sparring partner*
Balloon Cheeks
Slappy
Drummer

ENSEMBLE

Soldiers, factory workers, socialites, dancers, prize-fight crowd, children AND
  Chorus of singers in the orchestra pit

ACT I.   Scene 1

Left, a parachute factory, near a Southern town. Up left, a loading platform. At the back, a river. Right, trees and shrubs, with indications of an army camp beyond.

At rise: STEVEDORES *are loading cases on to the platform from the factory, preparatory to transferring them to river barges. M.P.'s are on guard. Others are gathered around a parachute, stage C., stretching it in preparation for folding. An aviation* OFFICER *looks on.*

SOLDIERS and WORKERS
[As the workers shift bales of silk in synchronization with the improvised song]

Send along anudder load
An' win dat war, win dat war!

FOREMAN
All right, gang! Fold it up!
[Workers fold parachute and load it into cart.]

SOLDIERS and WORKERS
One more to go an' den one more,
One more to go an' den one more,
   One more to go,
   One more to go.
Send 'em along an' win dat war!
Send 'em along! Send 'em along!
Send 'em along! Send 'em along!

1

[*Cart is wheeled into factory. The* OFFI-
CER *exits.* CINDY LOU *enters up C., looks
around, and starts to come downstage.*]

FOREMAN

Come on, gang! Start loadin' 'em in!

CINDY

[*To a workman at her R.*] Excuse me. Is dat de parachute factory over dere?

WORKMAN

Yeah, dat's it.

> [CINDY *crosses to the factory gate. As she
> tries to enter,* TWO SOLDIERS *on guard
> block the way. She then crosses down to
> look off L., then crosses C.*]

MORREL

[*To group R.*] Hmm! Hmm! Dat's for me!

> [MORREL, *the ladies' man of the crowd,
> very obviously adjusts his tunic, slicks
> back his hair, winks at his cronies, and
> approaches* CINDY *with elaborate gal-
> lantry.*]

WORKMAN

Ain' dat somethin'?

MORREL

Yes, sir! — Li'l gal, you look like you need help, an'
I feel like I kin help you.

CINDY

I wanna find a corpril —

[MORREL *ostentatiously thrusts out his arm displaying his corporal's chevron.* CINDY *smiles and shakes her head.*]
— Wanna find a corpril, name of Joe.

MORREL

Joe! We got thirty-seven corprils named Joe in dis out-fit. Gal like you orta find herself sumpin' more outa de ordinary. [*Primping*] What would you say if you was to meet a corpril named — Eustace!

CINDY

[*Naïvely literal*] Why — why, I'd say: "Pleased to meetcher, Eustace." I gotta go now. If you see Joe, will you say Cindy Lou was lookin' for him?

[*She starts to go, but* MORREL, *retaining her hand, holds her back.*]

MORREL

Cindy Lou!
[*Singing*]
Cain' let you go!
Before we let you go, we
Would like a slice o' sumpin' nice
Yore savin' up for Joey,
Oh, we —

ALL

Cain' let you go!
Before we let you go, we
Would like a slice o' sumpin' dat belongs to Joe!

[CINDY *laughs and shakes her head. She knows they mean no harm but she feels she must put them in their place.*]

3

CINDY

I'm a chick dat likes one rooster.
Never mess aroun' wid two.
Dat is why I mus' refuse ter
Be more den jus' perlite to you!
> [MORREL, *deflated, turns away. The
> others give him the horse laugh.*]

MEN

[*Spoken*] Jus' perlite!
Dat takes care o' you, boy!

CINDY

[*To console him, speaks*] I ain' sayin' dere's anythin'
wrong wid you, corpril.
> [*Singing*]
I like your eyes,
Your teeth are white an' snowy —
> [MORREL *is encouraged.*]
But when it comes to teeth an' eyes, dere ain' no flies
on Joey — oey!
> [*Another outburst of laughter as the* BOYS
> *repeat the refrain.*]

MEN

> [*With* CINDY — *the* MEN *taunting* MOR-
> REL]

She likes your eyes,
Your teeth are white an' snowy,
You's awful nice but not as nice as good ol' Joe!
> [SHE *runs off* L. *The* MEN *wave her away.*
> MORREL *looks disconsolate. When the
> bugle sounds he starts giving commands
> with special fierceness.*]

4

FOREMAN

Here it comes!
The change of guard!

MORREL

Come on — break it up! First squad — fall in. Dress
right. Dress ready front parade rest attention. Right
shoulder arms. Order arms!

> [*Silent* MANUAL *follows executed by both
> squads. The bugle call in the distance
> announces the approach of the guard re-
> lief. Those on guard line up. The* WORK-
> MEN *stop and look on as the relief marches
> on led by* SERGEANT BROWN, *and performs
> the brief but impressive ceremony of the
> changing of the guard.* JOE *is one of those
> in the new group. A line of* STREET UR-
> CHINS *march on like soldiers, carrying
> broomsticks, baseball bats, etc. As the
> following refrain is sung by the high
> SOPRANOS *in the manner of children, the
> CHILDREN perform the identical maneu-
> vers that the soldiers just executed, with
> perhaps a few slips for comedy relief.
> Perhaps there is a "Dopey" in the crowd.*]

CHILDREN and SOPRANOS

Lift 'em up an' put 'em down,
Lift 'em up an' put 'em down,
Mark time an' lift your tootsies,
Six inches off de groun'.

Lift 'em up an' put 'em down,
Marchin' all aroun' de town,

5

Comp'ny! Squads right!
Dat means turn aroun'!

Wish dat I was twen'y-one,
Ol' enough to tote a gun,
I'd go an' be a soldier —
Dere de ones dat have de fun!

Wisht I was a bugler man,
Playin' in de army ban'.
I'd blow it till I busted,
Playin' in de army ban' —

Ta ta ta ta ta ta ta
Ta ta ta ta ta ta ta ta, etc.

> [*After executing the guard change, they run off L. to a command of "Hey, Commandos!" from the* leader. DOPEY *remains behind, dreaming.* JOE *crosses to him — slaps his backside. He runs off after the others.*]

FOREMAN

[*To one of the new guards*] Hey, Joe! You know a gal name of Cindy Lou?

JOE

Sure do! Lives nex' door to me back home —

FOREMAN

Was aroun' here lookin' for you 'bout a minute ago.

JOE

Cindy Lou was here? What'd she come for?

FOREMAN

She got a nice pair of legs — a little skinny, but nice.

Eileen Darby — Graphic House

"LIFT 'EM UP AND PUT 'EM DOWN"

Act I. Scene 1

[SERGEANT BROWN, *who led the new guards on, saunters over to* JOE.]

BROWN

Hey, corpril — dis fac'ry we're guardin' — dey make par'chutes here, don't dey?

JOE

Da's right. Use ter be a cigarette fac'ry before de war. . . . You is new in de camp, ain't you, sergeant?

BROWN

I jus' been transferred down from New York.

JOE

New York! Da's a place I'd like to see.
[*A small* GROUP *has gathered near them attracted by* BROWN'S *swaggering manner.*]

BROWN

You prob'ly will — on de way over. An' I'm de one dat c'n show you de town. You like gals?

JOE

I — I guess I like 'em all right.

BROWN

You *guess* you like 'em! Da's a hot one!

1ST SOLDIER

Joe's got all de gals in dis fac'ry runnin' after him! Dey all tried to knock him off, but nobody got him, yet.

BROWN

Fer true? [*To* JOE] Why you ol' Casamova, you!
[*Big laugh from the* BOYS]

2ND SOLDIER

One gal in pertickler — a certain Miss Jones —

JOE

[*Sharply*] Da's enough 'bout dat!

1ST SOLDIER

Look how he flare up when you mention Carmen!

BROWN

Carmen? Sounds like a hot bundle. She good-lookin', Joe?

JOE

Yeh. She's good-lookin' I guess.

BROWN

Then why don't you give in to her? What you got to lose?

JOE

I — I already *got* a gal. My gal lives in anudder town.

BROWN

If you got a gal in anudder town, boy, you ain' got no gal at all!

> [*A big laugh goes up from the* MEN. *The factory whistle blows. The* WORKMEN *pick up their lunch boxes and gather in a group around the wagon, D.L., and start to sing.* BROWN *and* JOE *cross U.C.* FOREMAN *crosses to them.*]

MEN

Middle of de day,
People gettin' hungry.
Poor folks eat dere lunch,
Rich folks wine an' dine.
I don't wan' no lunch,

8

I ain' feelin' hungry.
I jus' wanna see dat honey gal o' mine —
Honey gal o' mine.
Honey gal o' mine.

> [*The last two lines of the song are hummed* bouche fermée *by the* MEN. *On the cue "Honey gal o' mine," laughter from the* GIRLS *is heard off L.*]

BROWN
[*Looking off L.*] Who dat dey makin' all de fuss 'bout?

FOREMAN
Das Eddie Perkins — *Lieutenant* Perkins now! Use ter work here right 'longside o' me!

JOE
Gee, I'd give my right arm to be a flier like him.

> [PERKINS *enters from the factory. The group of soldiers D.L. rise and salute him.* BROWN *and* JOE *salute him, too. As* PERKINS *crosses to C., the* FOREMAN *joins him, both cross D.R. The* MUSIC *changes and swells up as the* GIRLS *enter from the factory. Some of the* BOYS *wave their hats and shout to them. The* GIRLS *huddle and cast admiring glances at the officer. A* GIRL, *pushed forward by the other girls, approaches the officer shyly.*]

GIRL
Eddie —

> [*She looks back and starts to giggle. So do the others, but they encourage her to continue.*]

9

GIRLS

Go on an' say it!
Tell him like we *told* you!

GIRL

Lootenant — we hope if you ever *got* to use a parachute dat you use one o' de ones we made here.
[*The* GIRLS *sing to him.*]

GIRLS
[*Singing softly*]

Good luck, Mister Flyin' Man,
When you bail out,
When you bail out.
Jus' pull dat string —
Like a bird on de wing you will sail out.
Good luck while yore fallin' down
From above,
From above.
You'll reach de groun' —
It's as easy as fallin' in love.

Good-bye to silk stockin's an' silk underwear!
We gotta have silk dat kin float in de air.
Our paratroop fellers
Need yeller umbrellers,
De kind we know will get dem dere!
[*"Flyin' Man" Dance starts here.*]
Good luck, Mister Flyin' Man,
Flyin' man, floatin' down,
Floatin' through the blue —

Happy landin' to you,
Happy landin' to you,
Happy landin' to you!
Flyin' man . . . flyin' man.

> [*From "Flyin' Man" segué directly to* CARMEN's *entrance music. Someone looks off, sees her, and tells someone else. A whispered stir goes through the crowd. She enters. Two people are not impressed* — JOE, *who continues to clean his rifle, and a girl named* SALLY, *who speaks her mind.*]

SALLY

[*In between musical phrases*] Well, git a load of dat hip-swingin' fluzy, rollin' aroun' to work in time fer lunch!

> [CARMEN *stops in her tracks, turns and walks slowly over to* SALLY — *to music.*]

CARMEN

[*After musical phrase is ended*] Ev'y time you open dat ol' prune puss,
You make soun's I don' like.

SALLY

How we goin' to help de war effort if we don' git to work on time? You cain' help de sojers by stayin' home in your bed!

CARMEN

[*Flicking a speck from her bodice*] Dat's what *you* think!

SALLY

[*Stamping away toward the factory*] I'm goin' right inside an' tell de foreman on you!

CARMEN

[*Calling after her*] You do an' I'll scratch out de one good eye you got left!

> [SALLY *exits.* CARMEN *paces up and down angrily.*]

Help de sojers! Didn't I like to wear my feet out dancin' wid 'em at Billy Pastor's las' night?

A WORKER

How 'bout goin' down to Pastor's wid me tonight, Carmen?

BROWN

> [*Pushing him away, and addressing* CARMEN *confidently*]

I'm Sergeant Brown from New York, an' I don' waste no time.

CARMEN

You wastin' your time right now, boy.
[*Turning her eyes in* JOE's *direction*] De wind blowin' me in anudder direction.
[*Walking slowly toward* JOE] An' dere's no use arguin' wid de wind. . . .

> [T-BONE, *a very short and slender stripling, jumps in front of her.*]

T-BONE

Hey, Carmen, how 'bout goin' to Pastor's tonight wid your little frien' T-Bone? I c'n dance dose other boys right off de floor!

> [*He does a flashy step to show her.*]

CARMEN

[*Whose eyes have remained on* JOE] Uh-uh, T-Bone.
You're too little an' too late!

BOY

Well, look, Carmen, whyn't you pick out one of us an'
go stiddy, stid of all-a-time playin' de field?

GIRL

Yeh, pick out *one*. Dat'll *release* de rest o' dem!
[CARMEN *laughs.*]

CARMEN
[*Speaking, the music fitting metrically*]

I won' pick out de man —
An' he won' pick out me!
[*Singing, watching* JOE]
It don' go dat way,
You cain' ever know
Where your crazy heart wants to go. . . .

Love's a baby dat grows up wild
An' he don' do what you want him to,
Love ain' nobody's angel child
An' he won' pay any mind to you.
[*For the benefit of* BROWN, *who is still
"hanging around"*]
One man gives me his diamon' stud
An' I won' give him a cigarette.
[*Looking over at* JOE]
One man treats me like I was mud —
[*Coming closer to him*]
An' what I got dat man c'n get.

[*Singing "against"* CHORUS, *who sing:*
"*Love's a baby,*" *etc.*]

Dat's love . . . dat's love!
Dat's love . . . dat's love!

CHORUS

Love's a baby dat grows up wild
An' he don' do what you want him to,
Love ain' nobody's angel child
An' he won' pay any mind to you.

CARMEN

You go for me an' I'm taboo,
But if yore hard to get I go for you,
An' if I do, den you are through, boy,
My baby, dat's de end of you.

CHORUS

De end of you!

CARMEN

So take your cue, boy,
Don' say I didn' tell you true.

CHORUS

She tol' you true!

CARMEN

I tol' you truly,
If I love you dat's de end of you!
When your love-bird decides to fly
Dere ain' no door dat you c'n close.
She jus' pecks you a quick good-bye
An' flicks de salt from her tail, an' goes!
[*Going close to* JOE *again*]
If you listen den you'll get taught,

14

An' here's your lesson for today:
If I chase you den you'll get caught,
But once I got you I go my way!

Dat's love . . . dat's love!
Dat's love . . . dat's love!

CHORUS

When your love-bird decides to fly
Dere ain' no door dat you c'n close.
She just pecks you a quick good-bye
An' flicks de salt from her tail, an' goes.

> [CHORUS *joins her in final and climactic refrain.*]

CARMEN

You go for me an' I'm taboo,
But if yore hard to get I go for you,
An' if I do, den you are through, boy.
My baby, dat's de end of you.
De end of you.

CHORUS

De end of you.

CARMEN

So take yore cue, boy,
Don' say I didn't tell you true.

CHORUS

She tol' you true.

CARMEN

I tol' you truly,
If I love you dat's de end of you.

15

[*After the song* CARMEN *goes to a group of* GIRLS *who start to whisper to her, as the* MEN *go over and address* JOE.]

MEN
[*This is sung, with a lusty attack*]

Hey, Joe! Don' let her git her hooks into you!
Say, Joe! Don' do anythin' I wouldn' do!

[CARMEN *leaves the* GIRLS, *goes down to* JOE, *looks at him a moment, then impulsively taking a rose from her hair, she throws it straight at* JOE'S *heart. It hits him, then falls to the ground. The* GIRLS, *on the way back into the factory, pass* JOE *and sing to him, kidding him.*]

GIRLS
You go for me an' I'm taboo,
But if yore hard to get I go for you.
An' if I do, den you are through, boy,
My baby, dat's de end of you!

[*They go in and* CARMEN, *who has been watching him, now turns and runs off after them. The* MEN *move upstage and exit. The picture thins out.* JOE *is left alone with his confused thoughts and emotions. He looks down at the flower, gives it a little kick. Making certain no one is watching him, he stoops over, picks up the flower, and smiles down at it, when he hears* CINDY LOU'S *voice.* CINDY *enters from U.L.*]

16

HABANERA — "DAT'S LOVE"

Richard Tucker

CINDY

[*Seeing him*] Hey, Joe!

JOE

[*Turning quickly, holding the flower behind him, guiltily*] Cindy Lou!
> [*She runs to him, but his arms don't go out, so she stops short and becomes shy.*]

CINDY

S'prised to see me?

JOE

Sure am.

CINDY

I brought a letter from your Maw —
> [JOE *hastily puts the rose inside his tunic.* CINDY *gives the letter to him.*]

JOE

Thanks, Cindy.

CINDY

I ain' got no idea what's in it. . . .

JOE

How's my ol' lady feeling? She had any o' dem spells where she cain' get her breath?

CINDY

Not in a long while. Dr. Kirby say she gettin' better all de time —

JOE

Dat's good.
> [*Puts letter in his pocket.*]

CINDY

I come 'cause your Maw's been worried 'bout *you* —
dat's why I come.
[*Ominously*] Las' Sattidy she foun' two buzzard fed-
ders on de groun'!

> [JOE's *face clouds. Buzzard feathers are*
> *not to be taken lightly.*]

CINDY

She put a pan o' water on de doorstep in de moonlight
to keep de bad spirits 'way.

JOE

You don' believe in dat stuff, do you?

CINDY

No! An' I don' believe in tea leaves neither.

JOE

[*Pause. His voice is weaker*] De tea leaves been bad
lately, too?

CINDY
[*Singing*]

I tol' your Maw she's crazy to be frettin' —
But jus' de same
I up an' came.
I hopped a bus dis mornin',
Your Maw loan me carfare,
An' what she didn' say
To sen' me on my way —
A t'ousand millyun messages she give me for you!
I cain' remimber all — 'cepin' jus' one or two. . . .
Joe, your Maw say she awful lonesome,

But outside o' dat, she feelin' fine.
She say your cat is gittin' kittens —
It look like eight, an' maybe nine.
Den de nex' t'ing is hard to tell you.
> [*She looks away.*]
I'se inbarrassed as I kin be.
> [*She just can't face him.*]
She . . . she say: "When you see my Joey,
Give my Joey a kiss for me."

> [*They look at each other, both shy, both
> filled with inarticulate ecstasy. The music
> swells in a sweep of emotion, and that is
> how they feel. But all that actually hap-
> pens is that she walks over to him, stands
> on her toes, and gives him a quick, light
> kiss. Then she looks away. The music
> grows softer, the next three lines are
> spoken:*]

JOE
Dat wuz f'um my Maw?
> [CINDY *nods*]
It feel like it wuz f'um her. . . . You's de same kin'
o' woman as her. . . . You ain' like —
> [*His hand is on his chest, over the hid-
> den flower.*]

CINDY
Like who?

JOE
What I mean — you ain't like de kin' I wouldn't wan'
you to be. . . . You's like — like my Maw.

Carmen Jones

[*He looks at her earnestly, searching for
words. He finds them and he sings.*]

You talk jus' like my Maw,
You even walk jus' like my Maw,
An' I know why I'm stuck on you —
It's 'cause I'm jus' like my Paw!

CINDY

I talk jus' like yo' Maw,
I even walk jus' like yo' Maw,
An' I kin see why you like me —
'Cause you is like yo' Paw. . . .
You's awful like yo' Paw.

[JOE *hums obligato.*]

JOE and CINDY

Lemme tell you what de Lawd did:
He made you (me) live nex' door,
So we could fall in love
De way my (yo') Paw an' Maw did.

JOE

Is you my Cindy Lou?

[*He takes her in his arms.*]

CINDY

I is yo' Cindy Lou,
An' I belong to you.

JOE

An' I belong to you.
I am yo' Joe, my Cindy Lou,
An' I belong to you. . . .

[*After a pause of repose and content-
ment, in each other's arms,* JOE *suddenly*

20

*remembers the letter from his mother.
Takes it from his pocket and reads it. The
following lines are spoken:*]

JOE

'Scuse me while I see what she got to say.

CINDY

[*Suddenly scared because she knows
what his mother wrote*]

Yeh — you read it. I'll take a walk.

JOE

No. You stay. Won' take long.

CINDY

I'm thirsty.
[*Edging away*] I'll go over to de barbeque an' git a
coke. You meet me dere — if you wan' . . .

JOE

Cain' you wait a *second*?
            [*No, she can't. She's gone.* JOE *starts to
            read. His face lights up. He looks off, in
            the direction in which* CINDY *ran.*]
Well, what d'you know!
[*Reading, crossing D.R.*] "Furthermore I do believe
if you ast Cindy, an' if you ast her nice an' pretty,
you'd be standin' in front of a parson in no time!"
[*He looks off again.*] Well, what d'you know!
[*Reading*] "I would be proud to have her for my
daughter. I feel like she's my daughter already! Write
soon an' tell me what you think."

21

[*Folding letter*] What I think? I think dis de bes' idea you ever had, ol' lady. An' jus' in time, too!

> [*He takes the flower from under his tunic and is about to hurl it away from him when a terrific din comes from the factory. He looks around and forgets all about throwing the flower away.* PEOPLE *run from all sides.* SERGEANT BROWN *shouts to* JOE. *He cannot be heard above the babel but his gesture is clear. He points toward the factory, and* JOE *rushes in, fighting his way through a stream of* GIRLS *who are pouring out. During the song, the* MEN, SOLDIERS, *and* WORKMEN *run on, followed by the* KIDS, ALL *joining the excitement of the fight.*]

GIRLS
[*Surrounding* BROWN]

Murder! Murder!
Golly, what a gal!
Carmen! Carmen!
Got a-hold of Sal.
She got her by de throat,
She tearin' out her eyeballs!
Sal yellin' like a goat,
Don' wanna lose her eyeballs.
Wid Carmen tearin' out her hair
An' Carmen startin' in to bite,
Sal losin' all her clo'es,
Look like a holy sight!
Sal got a bloody nose!

22

Oh, baby! What a fight!
What a fight!
What a fight!
What a fight!

> [JOE *drags* CARMEN *from the factory.*
> *Running ahead, at a safe distance, is*
> SALLY, *looking sadly disheveled and*
> *angry.* CARMEN *bites* JOE's *hand. He lets*
> *her go for a second and she dashes after*
> SALLY, *who flees from her.* WORKERS *and*
> SOLDIERS *come between them.* JOE *gets*
> CARMEN *again and brings her down to*
> BROWN.]

BROWN

What you mean, actin' up dis-a-way?
[*To* JOE] What's de charge, corpril?

SALLY

[*Breaking in*] Murder! She try to choke me to death
an' —

CARMEN

I tol' you if you tol' on me I'd do what I tol' you I'd
do if you did!

SALLY

Go on back to de bad street you come off of!
> [*They now shout at each other.*]

CARMEN	SALLY
Who talkin' 'bout comin' off a bad street — you ol' hypocrite wid your big mouth, an' your jealous-	Go out yonder on de road an' play wid your kind! Comin' roun' here wid your biggidy ways an'

hearted ways! De only reason you git to work on time is 'cause all de men kick you outa bed soon's dey git a look at you. Git along, you fatal fool! Shut your evil-thinkin' fly-trap 'fore I ram my fist down your windpipe! rollin' your hips aroun' like a ol' river boat! You's a reckless strumpet an' a home-spoilin' rogue an' Gawd ain' goin' to be patient wid you! You know dat an' you know it good!

> [BROWN *claps his hand over* SALLY'S *mouth and* JOE *holds his over* CARMEN'S *mouth.*]

BROWN

Corpril, is you goin' to give me a report or ain' you?

JOE

Dis one was late comin' to work an' dat one tol' on her. Den dis one jump on dat one, an' when I come in, it look like she goin' to kill her —

> [JOE *breaks off because he becomes conscious of the fact, as he holds* CARMEN, *that she no longer resists him, but leans her head back against his chest and smiles contentedly.*]

BROWN

[*Noticing this also*] Lessee, Miss Jones, you're de gal dat acted so uppity wid me a little while ago. If you had of been more civil wid me den it mightn't go so hard wid you now. As it is, I got to dole out de full penalty of de law.

Act I. Scene 1

CARMEN

[She sings "at" BROWN *with cool defi-
ance. Then returns to* JOE's *side.]*

You ain' a police'm,
You ain' a police'm,
An' you c'n do nothin' to me.
You ain' a police'm,
You ain' a police'm,
Dee dum de di dee dum di dee!

BROWN

*[Who has taken out a little book and is
making notes in it]*

You'll sing on a different side o' your face when I finish wid dis report. Startin' up disorder on gov'ment
property an' hol'in' up de war effort. Maybe sabitage
for all I know!

CARMEN

[She crosses to BROWN, *circles him. As
she does this,* SALLY *runs from her into
crowd.* CARMEN *ends up at* JOE's *side.]*

You ain' a police'm,
You ain' a police'm,
An' you c'n do nothin' to me.
You ain' a police'm,
You ain' a police'm,
Dee dum de di dee dum di dee!

BROWN

I'll tell you what I *c'n* do to you — I c'n have you
t'rown into de guardhouse an' kep' dere till de police

25

come — an' I don' have to tell dem to come in a hurry,
either —
[*Significantly*] 'Less you decide to be nicer to me.

CARMEN

Won' it do jus' as good if I'm nice to Joe?
>[*She gazes up at the shifting and embar-
rassed eyes of* JOE. BROWN *is furious.*]

BROWN

Okay, if da's how it is. Off to de guardhouse you go.
An' Corpril Joe c'n be de man to take you, too.
[*To* JOE, *angrily*] An' you see dat she gits dere quick!
You hear?

CARMEN

[*In a cooing voice*] Arres' me, Joe.

BROWN

An' tie her up, so she cain' scratch or kill no more
people.

CARMEN

[*Softly*] Tie me up, Joe.

JOE

[*Uncomfortably*] Wid what?

CARMEN

>[*Unwinding the bandanna she wears on
her hair*]

Here, honey. Use dis.
>[*She hands* JOE *the bandanna. He looks
at it uncertainly.*]

BROWN

[*Shouting*] Well, go on an' tie her up. What you wait-in' for?

> [JOE *starts to tie her. There are murmurs and giggling from the crowd. And now, to their great amusement,* CARMEN *starts to sing to* JOE *as he ties her.*]

CARMEN

You go for me an' I'm taboo,
But if yore hard to get I go for you,
An' if I do, den you are through, boy,
My baby, da's de en' of you!

> [CARMEN'S *hands are tied. She runs from* JOE *to D.L.* BROWN *hands* JOE *his helmet and pushes him toward her.*]

ALL

De en' of you!

CARMEN

[JOE *crosses to* CARMEN] So take your cue, boy,
Don't say I didn' tell you true!

ALL

She tol' you true!

BROWN

[*To* JOE] Hey, Joe! Ketch.

> [JOE *turns.* BROWN *throws his notebook at him.* JOE *catches it.* CARMEN *thus gets the chance to sing the last phrase to* JOE *and "sell" it.*]

CARMEN

I tol' you truly,
If I love you, da's de en' of you!

[JOE *grabs her. She quite willingly starts
stage R. with him.*]

ALL

Dat's love!

[JOE, *holding* CARMEN, *crosses to C.*]

Dat's love!

[CARMEN *breaks away from him and runs
to R.C.*]

Dat's love!

[*As* JOE *runs to her to grab her, she kisses
him.*]

Dat's love!

[JOE *leads her off R. The* KIDS *fall in behind* CARMEN *and* JOE *and follow them,
laughing gaily. The* CROWD *shouts glee-
fully as the curtain falls on the scene. The*
PIT CHORUS *starts to sing,* a cappella.]

Entr' Scene

Carmen Jones is goin' to jail,
Carmen Jones is goin' to jail,
Carmen's gotta stay in jail
Sit all day upon her tail.
Carmen Jones is goin' to jail,
Is goin' to jail, is goin' to jail,
Hooray!

A CT I.   Scene 2

A road, lined with lush, tropical shrubs.

At rise: JOE *leads* CARMEN *on, followed by* EIGHT
KIDS. *They are singing tauntingly, "Carmen Jones is
goin' to jail!"* CARMEN *and* JOE *take swipes at the kids
and try to drive them back.*

JOE

Git away dere! Go 'long home now! . . . De first
thing you know *you'll* go to jail, too!

> [*He chases them away.* ONE LITTLE BOY
> *is too slow.* JOE *grabs him, gives him a
> whack on the pants, and sends him on his
> way. But this is a tough kid. He stops at
> the exit, shaking his fist at* JOE *and yell-
> ing in a piping voice:*]

TOUGH KID

I'll git even on you, you big lug!

> [*The* KID *runs off.* JOE *grins, turns, and
> to his surprise finds* CARMEN *seated on a
> rock, rubbing her ankle.*]

JOE

Come on, you! No sittin' down! 'Tain' but a quarter
of a mile to de guardhouse.

CARMEN

[*An appeal for sympathy in her voice*] Joey — I
turned my ankle jus' now, chasin' dem hellions. Guess
I must o' sprained it.

> [*Holding her leg up*]

Look! Looks like it's swellin' up, don' it?

30

JOE

I don't see no swellin'.

CARMEN

[*Rubbing her ankle*] It don' feel as sof' as de udder one. Feel it.
> [JOE *does. After all, he isn't made of iron.*]

Now feel de udder one.
> [JOE *sits beside her and does as she asks.*]

JOE

[*After touching the other one lightly*] Bofe de same!
> [*He takes off his helmet.*]

CARMEN

Listen, Joe, be a sport. If you put me in de guardhouse, what good c'n I be to you?

JOE

Quit it, now!

CARMEN

'Member dat flower I threw at you?
> [*Seeing it protrude from his tunic*]

I see you kep' it.
> [JOE *is embarrassed.*]

Li'l Carmen inside your coat now right nex' to your heart.

JOE

Come on, now — we got to git goin'.
> [*He rises and pulls her to her feet. She stands close to him.*]

31

CARMEN

Boy, but you're strong, de way you pulled me up jus'
like I was nuthin' — I bet you're a good dancer, ain'
you, Joe? Bet we could have fun if we went out tonight. I know a good place, too. Jus' outside o' town
— 'cross de railroad bridge, opposite de gas station —

[*She starts to sing, seductively*]

Dere's a café on de corner, run by my frien', Billy
    Pastor,
A spot where a man takes a lady when he wants to
    move faster!
Guess I'll go an' say hello to Pastor.

[*She moves away from him, he follows
her. She eludes him, but he catches up
with her.*]

How kin a lady drink alone?
How kin a lady dance alone?
No lady kin romance alone —
I oughta have a sweetie pie! —

De one I had I give de air to —
I threw his toothbrush out de door!

[*She moves away from him.*]

Now dat I'm free, my heart is sighin'.
I'm off de hook, an' lookin' for more!
Dozens o' fellers telephone me,
All axin' me to make a date.

[JOE *crosses to her — takes her arms.*]

I'm holdin' out for sumpin' special,
But I don' know how long I'll wait!

[*She moves away.*]

Where will I wind up?

32

Who'll I be true to?
> [*Coming closer to him*]

Ain' made my mind up —
Waitin' for you to!
> [*Leaning against his shoulder*]

Whatcher say, brudder?
Whatcher say, boy?
Ain' it time dat we got away?
> [*She leaves him as suddenly as she came
> to him, and resumes her refrain gaily and
> with expectant triumph.*]

Dere's a café on de corner, run by my frien', Billy
Pastor.
Dere's no way to know jus' how far I will go if I
has ter!
Maybe dat's a promise, maybe it's a threat!
> [JOE *crosses up away from her* — *she
> follows up to him.*]

JOE
> [*His voice not as strong as his words. His
> conscience is making a last stand.*]

Go away! Don' you know you don't dass talk to me?
> [JOE *sits on tree stump.*]

CARMEN
> [*Singing*]

Who say I talk to you?
> [*She moves away.*]

I'm singin' to myself —
Jus' singin' to myself.

33

An' I'm thinkin' . . .
> [*She moves to him*]

To think a little ain' 'gin' de law.
I'm thinkin' I oughta be wise
An' look in dat young sargint's *eyes*.
> [JOE *looks at her*.]

So dreamy,
So sweet an' dreamy
He'll wanta free me —
> [JOE *rises*.]

An' see me later on!
> [JOE *crosses to her — holds her arms*.]

But I don' wan' no sargint ef I kin have you,
Your arms are stronger den his.
> [JOE *takes away his hands*.]

Ef you take me out,
Dere ain' nuffin' dat's nice I won' do
> [*She turns to him*.]

I'll show you what a woman is!
> [*She turns away*.]

JOE
[*Floundering. Singing*]

Look here, is you tryin' to fool me?
Swear to Gawd you wouldn' fool me!
> [*He moves in close, hands on her arms.*
> CARMEN *knows she's got him now. So
> does he.*]

'Cause I'd free you,
If I could see you.
Say kin I see you!
An' out on de town we'll go!

34

CARMEN

[*A simple and direct girl*] Yes.

JOE

[*Unbinding her hands*] We got a date den?

CARMEN

See you at ten!

JOE

Where do we meet?

CARMEN

At Billy Pastor's.

JOE

Okay!

CARMEN

Don' keep me waitin' at Pastor's.
        [*She takes the bandanna from him.*]

JOE

I won' be late!

CARMEN

[*Crossing D.L.*] At ten o'clock sharp on de corner!
See dat you're right in dere pitchin' —
'Cause I ain' de kin' of a mare dat'll stan' widout
hitchin'!

> [*Her hands are untied. She hums gaily,
> waving the bandanna that bound them,
> blows* JOE *a kiss. He crosses to her. She
> eludes him and runs off. He looks after
> her, thinking of tonight at Billy Pastor's.
> From behind the trees come sounds of
> children giggling.*]

JOE

Who's dat? What made dat noise?

> [*He turns back and looks down the road*
> *toward* CARMEN. *He waves. The giggling*
> *starts again.* JOE *wheels around angrily.*]

Who *is* dat? Come out, whoever you are, er I'll shoot —

BROWN

[*Entering*] Who you shootin' at? What's goin' on
here? You talkin' at yourself?

JOE

Sargint, I —

> [*He breaks off, for following* BROWN *is*
> CINDY LOU.]

Cindy!

BROWN

Dis de feller?

CINDY

Yes, sargint.

BROWN

I foun' dis girl lookin' for you.

CINDY

What happened, Joe? You fergit all 'bout me?

BROWN

[*To* JOE] Seem like you copped all de good-lookin'
gals aroun' here.

> [JOE *signals* BROWN *to keep quiet, not to*
> *talk like that in front of* CINDY.]

D'you put the other one in the cooler?

> [*Giggles from behind the rocks.*]

Did you take her up before de lootenant?

KID'S VOICE
[*From behind tree*] He ain' take nobody to no cooler.
>CINDY *and* BROWN *turn.* JOE *looks as if*
>*he would like to vanish in air.*]

ANOTHER VOICE
He ain' take nobody up before no lootenant!

BROWN
Who de hell's makin' dat noise? Come outa dere!
>[*The* KIDS *come out from their hiding*
>*place.*]

TOUGH KID
[*To* JOE] I tol' you we'd git even on you, you big lug!
[*Turning to* BROWN] We was listenin' at them an' we
heared ev'ythin' they say.

BROWN
Everythin' who say?

ANOTHER KID
Him an' Carmen. She say if he let her go she'd meet
him tonight at Billy Pastor's.

ANOTHER KID
So he let her go!

TOUGH KID
She run down to dat udder road an' got a hitch from a
jeep.
>[BROWN *turns slowly toward* JOE. JOE
>*looks away.*]

BROWN

So, you disobey a superior an' you release your pris-
oner — an' what's worse, you go an' date up de pris-
oner.

> [CINDY, *deeply shocked and hurt, turns
> away.*]

Well, you ain' goin' t'keep no date tonight 'cause
you'll be in de guardhouse — and *I'll* be at Billy
Pastor's.

CINDY

Please don' do dat to him, sargint. Joe's a good boy.
He never spent one night in jail.

JOE

Cindy —

BROWN

[*Taking his arm*] He's goin' to spend more'n one night
dis time. Come on, boy.

JOE

You — you won' say nuthin' to my Maw, will you,
Cindy?

> [CINDY *bites her lip and shakes her head.*]

BROWN

Don' you worry 'bout what she tells your Maw. Better
worry 'bout what I'm goin' to tell de Lootenant.

> [BROWN *marches* JOE *off. Music swells
> up as* CINDY *stands looking at them while
> they exit. Then, alone, she sits on the rock
> and starts to sob. The* KIDS, *impressed
> and no longer mischievous, watch her in
> puzzled and awed silence.*]

A C T I.   Scene 3

Billy Pastor's Café. Three weeks later. The scene is
animated and noisy. Some are dancing, others are
standing at the bar or drinking at their tables. There
is a small bandstand on which a drummer is featured.
MYRT *and* DINK *are sitting at table L.* FRANKIE *and*
RUM *are dancing; through the opening music they*
dance toward the drummer. The music's "got"
FRANKIE. *She goes to the bandstand and starts singing.*

FRANKIE

I'll tell you why I wanna dance —
It ain' de sweetness in de music.
I like de sweetness in de music,
But dat ain' why I wanna dance!

It's sumpin' thumpin' in de bass,
A bumpin' underneath de music.
Dat bum-bum-bumpin' under music
  Is all I need
  To start me off.
  I don't need nuthin' else to start me off!

Beat out dat rhythm on a drum,
Beat out dat rhythm on a drum,
Beat out dat rhythm on a drum,
  An' I don' need no tune at all.

ALL

Beat me dat rhythm on a drum,
Beat me dat rhythm on a drum,

39

Beat me dat rhythm on a drum,
  An' I don' need no tune at all!
      [*"Drum Dance" — starts here.*]

FRANKIE

I feel it beatin' in my bones,
It feel like twen'y millyun tomtoms.
I know dere's twen'y millyun tomtoms
Beatin' way down deep inside my bones!

I feel it beatin' in my heart,
An' den I get a kin' o' dream
An' in my dream it kin' o' seem
Dere's jus' one heart
In all de worl' —
Dere ain't but one big heart for all de worl'.

  Beat out dat rhythm on a drum,
  Beat out dat rhythm on a drum,
  Beat out dat rhythm on a drum,
  Dere's one big heart for all de worl'.

ALL

Beat me dat rhythm on a drum,
Beat me dat rhythm on a drum,
Beat me dat rhythm on a drum,
Dere's one big heart for all de world'!

FRANKIE

An' now dat heart is beatin' fast,
An' dat's a rhythm I kin dance to,
I'm mighty glad I got a chance to,
Wid dat one big heart dat's beatin' fast!

Tomorrow mornin' let it rain,
Tomorrow mornin' let it pour,
Tonight we's in de groove together.
Ain' gonna worry 'bout stormy weather —
Gonna kick ol' trouble out de door!

Beat out ol' trouble on a drum,
Beat out ol' trouble on a drum,
Beat out ol' trouble on a drum,
An' kick his carcass through de door!

ALL

Beat out dat rhythm on a drum,
Beat out dat rhythm on a drum,
Beat out dat rhythm on a drum,
An kick ol' trouble out de door.
Kick 'im out de door!
Kick 'im out de door!
Kick 'im out de door!

> [*The last note ends in a shriek which co-
> incides with a shrill blast in the orchestra,
> and now the* DANCERS *whirl in a wild
> series of varied evolutions. The stage is in
> motion, all those not dancing indulging in
> whatever rhythmic eccentricities may be
> invented. It is a kaleidoscope of intense
> gaiety and passion. When it is over they
> flop into their chairs and on the floor and
> across the bar. After the dance is over the*
> DANCERS *slowly exit, others return to the
> tables and the bar.* RUM *leads* FRANKIE
> *back to the table.* DINK, *at table, whispers
> to* MYRT, *who laughs shrilly.*]

FRANKIE

[*As she sits, addressing* MYRT] What you two whisp'rin' about?

MYRT

He wan's me to go up to Chicago wid him.

FRANKIE

Dat's what Rum's been askin' me to do!
[*Turning to* RUM] Hey, Rum, you mean to say you'd take me an' Myrt all a way up to Chicago, fer true?

RUM

Fer true — and fer free!

DINK

All 'spenses paid! An' dat'd inclood some fancy noo clo's wouldn' it, Rum?

RUM

De bes' you can buy in de town!

FRANKIE

You hear what de man say, Myrt?

MYRT

Don' lissen at him. He's havin' a time wid you.
[MYRT *emits her shrill laugh again.* SERGEANT BROWN *comes up to the table.*]

BROWN

S'cuse me, Frankie — anybody see anythin' o' Carmen dis evenin'?

FRANKIE

Yeh, Carmen's here. Mus' be in de udder room.

Act I. Scene 3

MYRT

Sargint Brown, I'd like fer you to meet Mr. Rum
Daniels an' Dink Franklin.

BROWN

[*Uninterested, anxious to go and look for*
CARMEN]

How do, gen'lemen.

FRANKIE

Mr. Daniels is de manager of Husky Miller, de fighter.

BROWN

[*Impressed no end*] Oh, is dat so? Well, how do, Mr.
Daniels? Is Husky in town?

RUM

[*Conscious of his position as* HUSKY'S *manager*] Jus'
passin' through on de way up to Chicago.

BROWN

Is he in good shape to fight dat South American champeen?

DINK

He *will* be, boy, he *will* be!

[*He stops suddenly and his voice dies off
as* RUM *freezes him with a look. Then*
RUM *turns to* BROWN, *flicks an ash from
his cigarette, and puts the clincher on
everything.*]

BROWN

I'd sure like to see Husky. Dey tell me he's seven foot
tall.

43

DINK

Naw! He's only six foot six.
> [*Standing and holding his hand high above his head*]

Comes up to about here on me! . . . Rum discovered him unloadin' boats on Lake Michigan.

RUM

I see him comin' down a gangplank, carryin' a jeep on his back, an' I said: "Dat's my man!"

BROWN

Hope I see him when he comes here. Well, I guess I'll go look for Carmen.

FRANKIE

Won' do no good. She still sore at you 'cause you put Joe in de guardhouse for t'ree weeks.

BROWN

De t'ree weeks are up. He'll be out tonight.

MYRT

Den it *cert'nly* won' do you no good if *he's* comin' 'roun' here.

BROWN

We'll see 'bout dat.
> [*He exits into another room.*]

FRANKIE

Hey, Rum, honey, if you take us up to Chicago an' buy us a lot o' clo'es an' show us a good time, what *we* got to do fer you?

MYRT

Don' ask him dat *yet*. Git up to Chicago first!
> [*They all laugh loudly at this.*]

RUM

[*To* DINK] Tell you what, we'll take 'em to de club some Satiddy night!

DINK

[*Impressively*] He's talkin' 'bout de Meadow Lawn Country Club.

MYRT

Ain' dat de high-toned place where de Chicago swells go for de week-end?

DINK

[*Flicking an ash from his cigarette*] Yes, sir! Da's where we go!

FRANKIE

You a member?

DINK

N-no, but Rum is *tryin'* to be.

RUM

[*Conscious of the distinction*] My name is up. It's very 'sclusive but I 'spec' to make it.

DINK

Hey, Rum — if dey don' exclood *you*, what kind o' people *do* dey exclood?
[*A* BOY *and* GIRL *run on excitedly.*]

BOY

Husky's comin'! Husky Miller's comin'!

MYRT

[*Looking over his shoulder*] Hey, look! What's d' excitement?

45

[*There is a stir off U.L. Several people have left their tables and are looking through the door.* OTHERS *wait expectantly. There is the hum of whispers around the room and murmured ejaculations. As* OTHER COUPLES *come on running*]

A MAN

[*At the door*] Da's him all right!

> [HUSKY MILLER *enters and surveys the scene as if he owns it — and he does.*]

VOICES IN THE CROWD

Dere he is!

In de flesh!

Look jus' like his pitchers!

RUM

Dat's my boy!

> [*He rises and joins* HUSKY, *who is striding down majestically toward the bar.* DINK *follows* RUM, *leaving the* GIRLS *alone.*]

VOICES IN THE CROWD
[*To* HUSKY *as he passes*]

Goin' to win your nex' fight, Husky?

Goin' to knock out dat boy from Brazil?

Atta boy, Husky! You'll show 'im.

HUSKY

[*At bar*] Set up drinks for everyone.

RUM

Husky Miller's standin' treat fer de house!

DINK

De drinks are on Husky Miller!

VOICES IN THE CROWD

Oh, boy! D'you hear dat?
Well, ain' dat a *thing!*
Three cheers for Husky Miller, de comin' champeen
o' de worl'!
Hooray! Hooray! Hooray!

> [HUSKY *greets the crowd and strides
> downstage to respond to his public*]

HUSKY

Thanks a lot!
I'm sure glad to be,
To be where I c'n see
So many frien's o' mine.
How've I been doin'?
How've I been doin'?
If you really wanta know de truth,
I'm doin' fine!

DINK

Tell 'em, Husk!

HUSKY

Seventeen
Decisions in a row,
An' only five on points —
De res' was all K.O. . . .
Jackson an' Johnson,

47

Murphy an' Bronson,
One by one dey come,
An' one by one, to dreamland dey go!
How's it done?
You ask me, how's it done?
I got a trainer man
Who taught me all I know.
Sure feels good to have him in my corner,
Hear his voice a-whisp'rin' low:
"Big boy, remember,
You mus' remember. . . .

Stan' up an' fight until you hear de bell,
Stan' toe to toe,
Trade blow fer blow!
Keep punchin' till you make yer punches tell,
Show dat crowd watcher know!
Until you hear dat bell,
Dat final bell,
Stan' up an' fight like hell!"

[*Refrain is repeated by* ALL.]
[*During the interlude between this refrain and the next verse* CARMEN *enters.*
HUSKY *sees her and during the next verse
and refrain does a good deal of showing
off for her benefit.*]

HUSKY

When you fight
Out in de open air
In a patch o' light
De ring looks small an' white.

48

Out in de blackness,
Out in de blackness,
You c'n feel a hun'erd thousan' eyes fillin' de night!

Da's my boy!

Cigarettes
Are blinkin' in de dark,
An' makin' polka dots
Aroun' de baseball park,
People are quiet —
Den dere's a riot!
Someone t'rows a punch an' plants it right smack on
      de mark!

Somebody's hurt!
You kinda think it's you.
You hang across de ropes —
Da's all you want to do!
Den you look aroun' an' see your trainer's eyes,
Beggin' you to see it through,
Dey say, Remember,
Big Boy, remember —
> [*He repeats the refrain with full* CHORUS
> *support. Then* RUM *and* DINK *cross to him
> and take him to the bar.* BROWN *enters
> and approaches* CARMEN.]

Look, Carmen, you got no reason to be so uppity wid
me —

CARMEN

Go way f'um me, you Benedick Arnold!

BROWN

Carmen!

CARMEN

Go way 'fore I git Husky Miller to slap you down.
> [*She walks away. He starts to follow, but as she gets near* HUSKY *she turns back and looks at* BROWN.]

Wan' me to?
> [*After a pause,* BROWN *wisely decides to retire to another room.* CARMEN *continues past* HUSKY, *whose interest in her has remained continuous.*]

HUSKY

[*To* CARMEN, *as she passes by him*] Hey, Heat-wave!
> [*She stops and looks around.*]

Why'n't you come over an' interduce yourself to me?

CARMEN

Interduce myself? You talk like you know me already.

HUSKY

[*Going closer to her*] I noticed you de minnit you come in de room. . . . Did you notice me?

CARMEN

Why, no. You was actin' so quiet an' modest I didn' hardly know you was here.
> [*She walks away to join* FRANKIE *and* MYRT *downstage.*]

Fred Fehl

TOREADOR SONG: "STAND UP
AND FIGHT!"

RUM

[*Taking his arm*] C'mon, Husky — better come down to de train.

HUSKY

[*Looking wistfully toward* CARMEN] Train don' leave for an hour yet.

RUM

No, but it's waitin' in de station an' your berth's made up.

DINK

Gotta git your ten hours' shut-eye.

HUSKY

[*Pulling away from them*] I ain' sleepy —

RUM

'Member what you promised de trainer man!
> [*This is the one thing that can impress* HUSKY. *He pauses on his way towards* CARMEN, *thinks a moment, then comes back to* RUM *and* DINK.]

HUSKY

Okay. I ain' goin' to break no promises to *him*. But you two lissen to dis — an' lissen good! When I wake up tomorrer mornin' an' git off dat train —
[*Tossing his head toward* CARMEN] I wanna see Tootsie on de platform.

RUM

Her? S'pose she don' wanna go to Chicago?

51

HUSKY

Dat's *your* problem. All I say is, if you cain' show up
wid Tootsie, jus' don' come 'roun' at all! Go find yourself a new meal ticket.

DINK

But, Husk!

HUSKY

S'long, boys. Don' fergit what I jus' said.

> [*Waving to crowd as he goes up to door*]

[*Over their heads, to* CARMEN] I'll be seein' you, Heat-
wave! Good night, all!

CROWD

G'bye Husky!

Good luck!

We'll go down to de train wid you, Husky.

See dat you win your nex' fight!

Atta Husky!

Beat dat South American boy!

So long, boy.

> [*He goes out.* RUM *and* DINK *stand down-*
> *stage ruefully considering their trouble.*]

DINK

What's he mean — go find yourself a new meal ticket?

RUM

He means dat I don' eat. An', brudder, if I don' eat —
you starve!

> [CARMEN *looks after* HUSKY. FRANKIE
> *and* MYRT *talk to her as if continuing a*
> *conversation started before.*]

FRANKIE

[*Pointing to* RUM] Dat one is his manager. Dey wanta take Myrt an' me up to Chicago.

MYRT

Goin' to pay our fare an' put us up at a swell hotel!

FRANKIE

An' buy us clo'es an' fancy food an' drink.

MYRT

Girl, we'll be livin' on de fatheads of de land!

FRANKIE

[*Giving her a jab*] Sh! Dere comin'.

RUM

[*Coming over to them, followed by* DINK] Say, ain' it about time you babies was gittin' packed up?
[*Glancing sideways at* CARMEN, *sending up a tentative "trial balloon"*] An' while yore at it, might be a good idea to pack up your friend an' take her along, too.

FRANKIE

[*Her eyes gleaming*] Carmen?

DINK

Dat's who!

MYRT

[*To* CARMEN] You hear dat, honey? Dey want you to come to Chicago!

RUM

At de special invitation of Husky Miller!

FRANKIE

[*Shaking* CARMEN's *arm*] You hear what de man sayin'?

> [CARMEN's *face lights up and she seems
> to be considering the idea.*]

MYRT

Man! Will we have oursel's a ball!

RUM

All 'spenses paid by de management. Whaddye say, Tootsie?

> [*Singing*]

Wanna make a trip on de crack Chicago train?

FRANKIE

Now dat's a trip you oughta make —

MYRT

It won' be hard for you to take!

RUM

Trab'l 'bout as fast as a Kansas hurricane!

DINK

It only takes a half a day to be a thousand miles away!

CARMEN

[*A dream in her eyes*]

Away!

DINK

Come on!

FRANKIE

Away.

54

Act I. Scene 3

RUM

Come on.

MYRT

Away.

RUM, DINK, FRANKIE, and MYRT

Come on away!
Dat streamline injine won' delay!

CARMEN

Away!

DINK

Come on!

RUM

Come on!

MYRT

Away!

RUM

Come on!

FRANKIE, MYRT, and CARMEN

Away!

RUM and DINK

Come on!
Dat streamline injine jus' cain' wait,
Dat streamline injine ain' no freight,
Dat streamline injine won' be late!

> [*Their heads together, delivering a
> tempting "sales talk" to* CARMEN]

Whizzin' away along de track,
Clickety clack, clickety clack,

55

Leavin' de wind away in back,
Clickety clack, clickety clack,
Up a hill an' down a hill
An' out upon de plains agin,

FRANKIE and MYRT
Through a storm an' outa de storm
An' pretty soon it rains agin!

RUM and DINK
You hit a curve an' sway aroun',

CARMEN
[*They've "got" her*]
An' den you pass anudder town,

RUM and DINK
You curve de udder way aroun',

FRANKIE and MYRT
An' den you pass *anudder* town!

QUINTETTE
But you don' stop 'cause yore Chicago boun'!
You keep on roarin' down de road
An' keep on.
Leavin' de wind away in back,
Clickety clack, clickety clack
Up a hill an' down a hill
An' out upon de plains agin,
Through a storm an' outa de storm,
An' pretty soon it rains agin!
Only takes a half a day
To be a thousand miles away.

It only takes a half a day
To be a thousand miles away.
Away.

MYRT

Come on away.

QUINTETTE

Chicago!
Chicago!

MYRT

Come on away,
Away, away.

QUINTETTE

Come on away.
Come on away.
Hey!

MYRT

On a Chicago train!

QUINTETTE

On a Chicago train!

RUM

[*Speaking*] Go pack your duds — ain' got much time.

MYRT

Carmen'll come.

FRANKIE

I knowed she would.

DINK

Well, let's git goin'.

CARMEN

[*Singing*]

Wait! Lemme say my say. . . .
If you bustin' to go, den go,
But jus' count me out of de party.
Jus' count me out,
'Cause I ain' in!

CARMEN	RUM and DINK
Don' wan' no *part* of it,	Oh, Carmen, honey, have a heart.
Don' wan' no part of *it*,	Carmen you cain' run out on us.
Don' wan' no part!	Don' waste our time wid all dis fuss!
Don' wan' no *part* of it,	
Don' wan' no part of *it*!	FRANKIE and MYRT
Don' wan' no part!	Oh, Carmen, honey, have a heart.

DINK

What you got dat you like so much better den dis?

MYRT

Whaddye got?

MYRT and RUM

Whaddye got?

MYRT, RUM, and FRANKIE

Whaddye got?

MYRT, DINK, FRANKIE, and RUM

Whaddye got?

CARMEN

If I tol' you you'd only laugh.

MYRT

Oh, no.

DINK

Not me.

FRANKIE

Go on.

RUM

Give out.

CARMEN

You got to promise not to laugh —

DINK and MYRT

Okay.

FRANKIE and RUM

Okay.

CARMEN

[*Soulfully*] Dere's a man I'm crazy for!
              [*They* ALL *break their promise and start
              to laugh uproariously.*]

DINK

[*Spoken*] She got a man she crazy for!

FRANKIE

[*Spoken*] So she cain' come to Chicago!

RUM

[*Spoken*] Da's a laugh!

CARMEN

[*Earnestly, singing*] I'm in love — an' dat ain' no
laugh.

59

[RUM *and* DINK *put their arms around each other and sing in a mock-romantic manner.*]

DINK
Well shut my mouf an' call me dumb!

RUM
An' beat me! I'm a kettle-drum!

RUM and DINK
De birdies in de trees are hummin'
Carmen's in love,
Carmen's in love!
Still we ask: "Won' you come?
An' break your date, give de gate to your chum."

[CARMEN *laughs, and answers the question in the spirit in which it is asked.*]

CARMEN
[*Singing*]
Anudder night I might've come
To raise some pandemomium
But now de mockin' birds are hummin':
"Carmen's in love,
Carmen's in love!"
Leave me here wid my Joe,
An' take your train to Chicago an' go.

RUM
We gotta git you on dat train!

CARMEN
Some udder time.

Act I. Scene 3

RUM

What makes you think dere'll be anudder time?

ALL

What makes you think dere'll be anudder time?

RUM and DINK

To git a trip —

FRANKIE and MYRT

To git a trip —

RUM and DINK

To Illinois —

FRANKIE and MYRT

To Illinois —

RUM and DINK

An' git it free!

FRANKIE and MYRT

An' git it free!

CARMEN

[*Wavering, apparently*] Dat is a place dat I'd sure like to see. . . .

> [*Her friends pounce on her indecision quickly with a repeat of the "sales talk" refrain.* CARMEN *joins and the song is finished in a sweep of enthusiasm.*]

ALL

Whizzin' away along de track,
Clickety clack, clickety clack,
Leavin' de wind away in back
Clickety clack, clickety clack.

Up a hill an' down a hill
An' out upon de plains agin,
Through a storm an' outa de storm
An' pretty soon it rains agin!
Only takes a half a day
To be a thousand miles away.
It only takes a half a day
To be a thousand miles away.
Away.

MYRT

Come on away.

ALL

Chicago!
Chicago!

MYRT

Come on away,
Away, away.

ALL

Come on away,
Come on away,
Hey!
Whizzin' away along de track
Off to Chicago, Illinois!

> [*After the refrain* CARMEN *crosses D.R.*
> RUM *crosses to her.* MYRT, FRANKIE, *and*
> DINK *wait to see what* CARMEN *will do.*]

RUM

Whaddye say? You comin' wid us?

> [*Pause. Then* CARMEN *smiles and shakes
> head.*]

CARMEN

Uh-uh!

> RUM *and* DINK *look ruefully at each other.*]

FRANKIE

Maybe she change her mind when she git a secon' look at Joe!

MYRT

Maybe Joe ain' goin' show up a-tall!

> [RUM *motions to the others to leave him alone with* CARMEN.]

FRANKIE

Hey, Carmen, something tells me Chicago is going to be good for you!

DINK

Something tells me you're going to be bad for Chicago!

> [*They exit.* RUM *takes* CARMEN'S *arm and becomes confidential*]

RUM

Look, baby, le's talk plain. Tomorrer mornin' I gotta perduce you in Chicago — an' I don' care what it costs me!

> [CARMEN *laughs and walks away. He follows her with another argument.*]

I don' care what you do wid Husky — or what you *don'* do.

After you get dere if he don' 'peal to you, dat ain' my fault.

63

CARMEN

It ain't dat he don' 'peal to me. He jus' happen to ring my bell when I was busy.

RUM

Busy! Foolin' aroun' in a place like dis when you get a chance to go to Chicago. What you doin' here anyway, a smart chick like you, workin' in a fac'ry?

CARMEN

You gotta work if you wanta eat.

RUM

Not in Chicago.

CARMEN

No? What dey do dere?

RUM

A pretty gal like you don' have to do nothin' hardly. I could get you into a floor show. You'd prob'ly start off at a hundred a week.

CARMEN

A hundred dollars?

RUM

Sure. An' what've you got to do? Sing a little song. Shake a few things, finish up wid a bump, den walk off an' collect your salary.
[*Pause.*]

CARMEN

[*Thoughtfully*] I always wanted to go to a big town.

RUM

You belong in a big town! You too sharp for dis place. A gal like you needs room to swing herself around!

Dis town is strickly "sleepytime down South," "ama-choor night in Dixie"!

CARMEN

Sure. Da's all it is.

RUM

You goin' to stay here an' sleep or are you goin' to wake up an' come wid us?
> [*Pause.*]

CARMEN

I cain' tell you jus' yet —

RUM

I'll call back for you on our way to de station.

CARMEN

Okay. You do dat.

> [RUM *leaves.* CARMEN *paces the stage thoughtfully. A trip to Chicago isn't to be sneezed at. If only* JOE *would come too! She saunters over to a group of* SOLDIERS *at the bar. They are laughing with* BAR-TENDER.]

S'cuse me, boys. Wanna know sump'in 'bout army rules. S'pose a so'j'er get tired an' feels like takin' a rest. S'pose he wan's to make a little trip — say to Chicago. Who he ask?

A SOLDIER

He ask his commandin' officer.

CARMEN

An' what de commandin' officer say?

GLOOMY SOLDIER

He say *no*!

[CARMEN *starts to go, then turns back.*]

CARMEN

I get it. . . . Thanks.

1ST SOLDIER

Don' mention it. I might wanna ax *you* a question some time.

GLOOMY SOLDIER

An' de answer is *no*!

[*The* MEN *laugh and exit L.* CARMEN *turns away, then stops in her tracks, because, looking up at the staircase C., she sees her man,* JOE, *standing on the steps and scanning the room in search of her.*]

CARMEN

Joey!

[*He sees her and his face shines with joy. He comes down C. to greet her.*]

JOE

I was skeered you wouldn' be here.

CARMEN

Been here every night, waitin' for you to come.

[*From behind his back he produces a box of candy. She takes it with a squeal of delight.*]

CARMEN

Marshmeller fudge!

[*She leads him down L. to a table.*]

66

JOE

[*His face clouding*] What you do here every night?
Dance wid all de so'jers, I bet!

CARMEN

[*Enjoying this*] I had myself a coupla dances.
[*Laughing*] I do b'lieve he's jealous!

JOE

Mebbe I am. So what?
      [*He rises.*]

CARMEN

[*Pressing him gently back into chair*] Go easy, ol' boy.
Go easy. I didn' dance wid nobody I keer 'bout. Been
savin' all my dancin' fer you. You jus' set dere an'
Carmen'll dance fer you like you was a sultan er
sump'n.

        [CARMEN *starts to dance a slow, sinuous*
        dance. The following lines are spoken in
        rhythm, counter-metrically to the music:]
Thinkin' 'bout you all de time
While you was away from me.
        [*She hums and dances closer.* JOE *is*
        fascinated.]
I been dreamin' 'bout tonight,
Wonderin' if you would be
Feelin' half as lovin'
As your Carmen feels for you!
        [BARTENDER *enters from D.R. and crosses*
        to C.]
Hey, Pete! Bring a couple o' rum cokes for me an' my
friend.

BARTENDER

Okay!

> [*He goes to the bar.* CARMEN *continues her dance. She hums again. Bugle motif in orchestra.* JOE'S *face clouds.*]

JOE

Carmen —

CARMEN

[*Continuing to dance*] What is it, honey?

JOE

[*Swallowing hard, not knowing how to phrase the bad news*] Gotta tell you sump'in.
[*Rises, moves to table, sits on it.*] It took me 'mos' a hour to git here from de camp.

CARMEN

> [*Sitting on table beside him, patting him and improvising a little chant, spoken, not sung, to the melody*]

Poor chile! Never mind —
Carmen take him home wid her,
Carmen will unlace his shoes
An' send him off to sleep.

JOE

[*How he'd like not to say this!*] Well, da's jus' it! Dey only give me a short leave. I gotta git de nex' bus back to camp.

CARMEN

[*Stunned*] Are you kiddin'?
[*Walking away, angrily*] Are you kiddin'?

JOE

No. I ain't kiddin'.

CARMEN

Boy! Ef dis ain' one on Carmen!

> [JOE *rises.* BARTENDER *crosses to* CAR-
> MEN *with glasses.*]

Boy! Ain' dis a joke on Carmen!

> [JOE *sits on chair R. of table.*]

I t'row myse'f about
An' dislocate a hip,
An' wear my girdle out
To in'ertain a drip!

> [*This is addressed to* BARTENDER. *He
> looks at* JOE, *places glasses on table, and
> exits.*]

I wuz gay! I wuz bright!
An' oh, what pretty plans
I cooked up fo' tonight!

> [JOE *rises — crosses to her*]

Go on an' git your bus!
But dat's de end of us!
[*Turning on him savagely*] Get along, droopy
drawers!
[*Crossing to table L.*] Go on back to de camp, lay on
your bunk an' look up at a pin-up gal — see what *dat*
gets you!

> [A COUPLE *enter from R. in time to hear
> following.*]

[*Throwing his hat at him*] Take yo' ol' hat!

> [*Music swells and breaks.*]

69

[*Throwing box of candy*] An' yo' marshmeller fudge!
     [*Music punctuates. The* GIRL *runs off L.*
     above bar; the BOY *stands watching*]
[*Crossing to* JOE] An' git yo'self outta here.
[*Crossing to the bar*] I got some lost time to make up!
     [*Turns and shouts across at the* BOY, *who*
     entered in time to duck the missiles]
Hey, boy! . . . Hey, you! . . . Come here!
     [*The* BOY *crosses to her. She crosses*
     toward JOE]
I want yo' to have a rum coke wid me!
     [*The* BOY, *thus accosted, joins her; they*
     move to the chair R. of table; she sits on
     his lap and passes him a glass, taking the
     other one for herself. They laugh.]

JOE

[*Taking a step toward them*] Carmen . . . I wanna
talk to yo'.
     [*When she does not answer, he crosses to*
     her and grabs her by the shoulders.]
Yo' gotta lissen!
     [CARMEN *rises sharply and crosses in*
     front of table to D.L. JOE *crosses to her*
     above the table, to her L.]
Look, Carmen!
     [*The* GIRL *who entered with the* BOY CAR-
     MEN *is entertaining now returns from the*
     L. and crosses down to him. As he sees her
     he quickly rises and they both exit U.L.,
     she wildly pantomiming "What the hell
     goes on here?" CARMEN *crosses to chair R.*

of table and sits. JOE *crosses to her, above
the table, moves a chair down to her R.,
and sits. She turns away from him. He
speaks softly:*]

I want you to see sump'n.

[*She turns slowly. He takes from the
breast pocket of his shirt the faded flower
she gave him three weeks ago. She is impressed in spite of her impatience with
him. Yet, perversely, she looks away
again. She doesn't want to be taken in by
sentiment. All she knows is that their evening, so long anticipated, is spoiled, and
somehow she feels it is his fault. He's
failed her.* JOE, *to convince her she's
wrong, now lets his heart out, with all
defenses down and the brakes released.
During the refrain* CARMEN *can't help being affected by his sincerity, and she
softens visibly.*]

JOE

Dis flower dat you threw my way
Has been my frien' by night an' day.
I saw it fade an' lose its bloom,
But still it kept a sweet perfume.

[CARMEN *rises, crosses to C.* JOE *rises —
stops her.*]

In my cell, through ev'ry darkened hour,
On my lonely eyes lay dis flower.

[CARMEN *crosses to bandstand steps —
sits.*]

71

An' so I'd sleep de whole night through,
> [JOE *crosses to her.*]

An' dream of you, an' dream of you!
> [CARMEN *uses compact to make up face.*]

Den I'd wake up, wid no one near me,
An' talk fo' de jail walls to hear me —
"She ain' de bes',
Dere all de same!
Like all de res'
She jus' a dame!"
> [CARMEN *closes compact.*]

Den I tol' myse'f I wuz ravin',
Dere wuz jes' one t'ing I wuz cravin' —
It wuzn' food,
It wuzn' dough!
I guess you know
Dat it wuz you!
> [CARMEN *moves away from him to C.* JOE
> *stops her.*]

I only saw you once.
Once wouldn' do!
I don' know anythin' about you.
I don' know much about a shinin' star.
Jus' know de worl' is dark widout you —
Das' all I know. . . .
> [CARMEN *moves away from him.*]

I only wan' you as you are. . . .
> [JOE *crosses to her.*]

Das' how I love you.
> [CARMEN *turns slowly to face him. Now
> that* JOE *has poured his heart out,* CAR-
> MEN *knows she can do pretty nearly what*

FLOWER SONG: "DIS FLOWER
DAT YOU THREW MY WAY"

she wants with him, and that the way to
keep control is to keep him guessing. So
she pretends not to believe him.]

CARMEN
[Shaking her head, walking away]

No. . . . Dat don' ring so true.

JOE
[Following her] I swear it's true!
[Puts flower away in tunic pocket.]

CARMEN
[Softly, crossing him to C.]

Joe, if you loved me true,
[She breaks suddenly into dialogue and
"gives it to him quick"]
You know what you'd do? You'd come to Chicago
wid me!

JOE
[He can't have heard right] Chicago?

CARMEN
I got enough dough to get us both dere.
[She crosses to JOE.] Been savin' up to give my man
a time when he got outa jail.

JOE
But, Carmen — why Chicago?
[BARTENDER enters from U.L., crosses to
bar.]
Chicago?

73

CARMEN
[*Singing seductively*]

If you would only come away,
If you would hide away wid me,
You would be where you wanna be,
Wrapped in your Carmen's arms from day to day —
Come away, Joey. Hide away. . . .
[*Speaking*] You cain' have no fun in a place like dis
— ev'ybody knowin' you an' watchin' what yore doin'.
Chicago would be like livin' outa dis world . . . all
by oursel's!

JOE
Yeh, but, honey — I'm in de army!

> [BARTENDER *crosses to tables R., clears*
> *glasses, returns to bar*]

CARMEN
[*Singing*]

I don' wan' you bustin' yore arm,
Totin' a army rifle, an' dat is a fac'!
Yore arm musn' come to no harm —
Pore little Carmen needs it to hold up her back.

> [CARMEN *takes his arm and draws it*
> *around her waist.*]

Couldn' we have oursel's a time?
Nobody dere but you an' me,
You an' me, honey, would dat be bad?
All alone like Romeo an' Venus?

> [BARTENDER *crosses R., picks up hat and*
> *candy box, exits R. Pause. Then she*
> *speaks. A* BOY *and* GIRL, *arm in arm,*
> *enter R., cross stage, exit L.*]

74

Ah, Joey, I wanna go someplace where you's de las' thing I see ev'ry night an' de firs' thing I see ev'ry mornin'.

> [*The music dies down and drifts away. They remain in each other's arms. She releases him. He walks away.*]

JOE

Cert'nly would be a nice trip to make some time.

> [*He crosses to chair R. of table L., sits.*]

CARMEN

[*Crossing to* JOE] *Some* time! You can make it right now —tonight!

JOE

Tonight?

CARMEN

Sure. . . . All you gotta do is figger out some excuse to get away. Tell your captain your ol' grandmaw is dying.

JOE

My ol' grandmaw is dead!

CARMEN

De captain don' know dat.

JOE

I don' like to tell lies to de captain.

CARMEN

[*Mimicking him scornfully*] He don' like to tell lies to de captain! Boy, da's a lover, dat is!
[*Pacing the stage angrily*] Got a chance to go to Chi-

cago wid me — *on my check*! An' he cain' tell a lie!
Boy! Are you hot for Carmen! You jus' burnin' up wid
passion! . . . You sizzle! Like a fish on ice!

> [SERGEANT BROWN *enters.* SERGEANT
> BROWN *has been drinking.*]

JOE

Look, honey, you don' unnerstand how 'tis in de army.
I cain' afford to have no more black marks against me.
I'm tryin' to git into de officers' Flyin' School.

CARMEN

Officers' Flyin' School! Well, go ahead! Who's stop-
pin' you? Go on away to de school . . . an' be de
teacher's pet, for all I care. . . . Only don' fly back
here, da's all. You too chicken-hearted for me to was'e
my time on.

BROWN

[*Coming forward*] Flyin' School! Who's goin' to be a
flier? Caspar Milktoas'?

CARMEN

Caspar Milktoas'! Da's a good one!

BROWN

Lootenant Caspar Milktoas'!

> [CARMEN *screams with laughter.*]

Look at him! What a fine hunk of officer material *dat*
is!

JOE

[*Scowling dangerously*] You leave me alone, you
hear?

BROWN

Got 'bout as much chance o' bein' a officer as a flea inside your shirt. [*He yanks* JOE'S *shirt up from out of his trousers.*]

JOE

[*Sharply, as he tucks his shirt in*] Quit dat!

BROWN

[*To* CARMEN] Dat de feller you been waitin' fer to come outa jail? Da's no kind of a man for you, Carmen. Cain't even keep his shirt in his pants!

> [*He pulls* JOE'S *shirt out again.* CARMEN *giggles. This, as every man knows, is a very annoying thing under any circumstances, but with your best girl laughing at you, it puts murder in your eye.*]

JOE

You do dat agin' an' I'll —

BROWN

You'll what? . . . You ain't figgerin' on strikin' a s'perior officer I hope. Dat wouldn' be no little matter of three weeks in de guardhouse. More like three years.

JOE

Well — jus' leave me be, da's all.

BROWN

> [*Swaggering up to* CARMEN *and putting his arm around her*]

Hey, Carmen, what're you an' me goin' to do while

77

Joe's at de Flyin' School? Same t'ing like we been
doin' de pas' three weeks?

> [*He winks at her.*]

CARMEN

[*Giggling ambiguously*] Same t'ing!

> > [*All that* BROWN *says is convenient to her
> > purpose — stirring* JOE'S *jealousy, mak-
> > ing him forget everything but her. She
> > crosses to R., ignoring him.*]

JOE

Carmen — have you been seein' dis feller?

BROWN

What you so sore 'bout, Caspar Milktoas'?

JOE

[*Wheeling around savagely*] You stop callin' me dat!

CARMEN

Well, if you *ain'* a Caspar Milktoas', why you stand
dere lettin' him have a time wid you?

BROWN

Whatsa use o' kiddin' oursel's, Joe? You an' me both
swimmin' in de same pond, an' de pond ain't big
enough for two. Somebody's gotta get out — an' it
better be you!

> > [*He punctuates the last sentence by yank-
> > ing* JOE'S *shirt out again. That's it! There
> > is no deliberation behind* JOE'S *next
> > move. It is just a matter of reflex. He
> > hurls himself on* BROWN. *He picks up the
> > chair nearest him and swings it down on*

78

BROWN's *head.* BROWN *falls and lies on
the floor unconscious.* JOE *swings to hit*
BROWN *again, but* CARMEN *stops him.*]

CARMEN

Joe, stop dat! You'll kill him!
[*Awed by the sudden violence and its re-
sult.*]
Look like maybe he been hurt bad.

JOE

[*In a dull, stunned voice*] Yeah.

CARMEN

Three years for hittin' a s'perior officer — ain' dat
what he said?

JOE

Maybe more — if he's hurt bad.
[BARTENDER *enters from U.R. with tray.*]

CARMEN

[*Seeing him — with sudden decision*] Pete! Get him
outta de way — quick!
[*He stands staring at* BROWN *on the
floor.*]
Come on! . . . Come on, man!
[*He runs to the bar and drags* BROWN *behind the bar, out of sight.*]
[CARMEN *crosses to* JOE.] You an' me is headin' for
dat train.

JOE

No! If I go away da's desertin' —

79

CARMEN

If you stay here, dat's prison! What you got to lose?

JOE

Somebody'll find him dere.

CARMEN

[*Walking him down to the bandstand D.R.*] *Maybe* — but by dat time you an' me goin' to be *far* away, honey — *far* away!

> [3 SOLDIERS *enter U.R.*, GIRLS *on their arms, saying good-bye.*]

A SOLDIER

Hey, Joe! Ain't you comin' back to camp?

A SOLDIER

Bus leavin' in 'bout two minutes.

> [JOE *looks uncertainly at* CARMEN.]

A SOLDIER

Better kiss your honey an' run like hell!

CARMEN

He ain' goin' back to camp. Didn' you hear de news?

A SOLDIER

What news?

CARMEN

[*Sorry she brought it up*] Er — 'bout . . . [*Getting an inspiration*] 'Bout de officers' Flying School!

SOLDIER

Dey takin' you, Joe?

CARMEN

Dat's where he's goin'.

SOLDIER

[*Turning back to newcomers entering*] Did you hear dat? Joe's goin' to de Flying School!

SOLDIER

Hot diggety!
[*Crossing to* JOE] When did you get de word, Joe?
        [*More* PEOPLE *pour in and hang on his words.*]

JOE

I . . . why . . . I . . .

CARMEN

He got de word tonight. I was de firs' one he tol'.

A GIRL

Joe's goin' to be a officer!

A GIRL

Well, what d'you know?

SOLDIER

You know what dis means? We got a boy from our outfit goin' to be a officer!

ANOTHER SOLDIER

In six months he'll be a lieutenant!

GIRL

Maybe dey'll make him a captain!

SOLDIER

Tell dat bus to wait a minute.

SOLDIER

Dis calls for a celebration.

SOLDIER

We gotta drink to dis!

SOLDIER

Roll out de barrel!

SOLDIER

Hey, Joe! How 'bout makin' a speech?

AD LIB

Dis calls for a speech!
C'mon Joe! A speech!
Speech! Speech!

GIRL

Come on, Joe! Make a speech!
> [*They bring a chair down to him L.C. and try to put him on it. He shakes them off.*]

JOE

I don' feel like makin' no speech.
> [*He glares at* CARMEN. *She got him into this.*]

CARMEN

He's too modest —

MORREL

[*On the bandstand.* ALL *turn to him*] Hey! . . . *I'll* make a speech.
> [CROWD *ad libs and cheers.*]

CARMEN

[*Crossing toward him*] Da's right, Eustace. You make a speech. You's a sweet- talkin' man.

GIRL

Say it right, Eustace!

MORREL

Ladies an' gen'lemen, I'm talkin' 'bout Joe! Corpril Joe — soon to be Lootenant Joe!

> [*The* CROWD *cheers.* JOE *looks miserable.*]

Joe, we'se all proud of you 'cause you ain' de kind o' feller talks 'bout what he's goin' to do. You goes an' does it.

GIRL

Goes an' does it! Da's what he did!

> [*The* CROWD *cheers.* JOE *gets up on chair near him, holds up his hand, and shouts:*]

JOE

Hey! Look! Wait a minute. I gotta tell you somethin'. . . . De fact is . . . de truth is —

CARMEN

> [*On the bandstand, breaking in quickly, her voice tense*]

De truth is if Joe don' hurry an' make dat train, he won' get to de school. Dis your las' chance — ain' it, Joe?

> [*Coming off the bandstand, crossing toward him, speaking more slowly*]

If you don' go dere tonight, de army'll send you some‑ wheres else — won' dey, Joe?

> [*Pause.* JOE *steps down off the chair.*]

J O E

Yeah . . . I . . . I guess I better get to de train.

> [*This decision is the turning-point in his life.*]

C A R M E N

[*Crossing to him and taking his hand. Sings*] Joey, it's time for you to go.

J O E

Good-bye, now!

A L L

Lots o' good luck, Lootenant Joe!
Good-bye, now!

> [*A long line of* FRIENDS *forms quickly and through the singing each bids* JOE *good-bye, the* MEN *shaking his hand and clapping his shoulder, the* GIRLS *kissing and embracing him.* OTHERS *wave to him.* RUM, DINK, FRANKIE, *and* MYRT *enter from the center stairs when the singing starts, the* MEN *carrying suitcases. They cross down L.R.C. breaking through the crowd. When* CARMEN *sees them, she crosses to them to tell them that she is going with them. The* SOLDIERS *step forward and embrace* JOE. *As he breaks away from them he turns to see* CARMEN *waiting for him. He goes to her and hand-in-hand they move to the center stairs. The* QUARTET *follow them.*]

When you are flyin' far away
All o' your friends'll hope an' pray

By night an' day we'll pray!
So go an' do de bes' you can,
'Cause da's as good as any man can do!
Jus' go an' do de bes' you know,
An' we'll be proud, proud of our Joe!

> [*They all wave to him as he goes up the
> stairs with* CARMEN, *and the* CURTAIN
> FALLS.]

A c t I I.　　Scene 1

The Meadow Lawn Country Club, south side of Chi-
cago. Two weeks later. Night. The clubhouse extends
off R. from R.C. A shrub-lined, curving walk starts
from the house and continues down to extreme L. D.L.
is a small card table, two chairs, and a wrought-iron
bench.

　　At rise: The stage is draped with well-dressed folk.
A liveried STEWARD *serves drinks. This atmosphere*
of gentility presents a sharp contrast to the strident
exuberance of Billy Pastor's, many miles south.
Snatches of polite conversation and well-modulated
laughter are heard above the music.

HIGGINS
　　[To successive arrivals as they come
　　through the door to him]

Did you enjoy your dinner, Mrs. Dill? So glad you
could come. . . . And Mr. Gaines! I saw you sink
that thirty-foot putt today. Mrs. Vandunk! That hat
is too, too . . . too really!

　　　　[To RUM *as he enters with* MYRT *and*
　　　　FRANKIE]

Ah, Mr Daniels, welcome to Meadow Lawn Country
Club!

　　　　*[*RUM *smiles, bows, and shakes his hand]*
　　　　[Indicating FRANKIE]

And is this Mrs. Daniels?

　　　　*[*FRANKIE *tugs at* RUM'S *sleeve in embar-*
　　　　rassment. HIGGINS *senses his faux pas and*

86

FINALE—ACT ONE

Richard Tucker

*turns to greet other guests coming from
the house.*]

RUM

[*To girls after they have crossed* HIGGINS] Honey!
He's regular. . . . Dat's Mr. Higgins, de president of
de club.

MYRT

Sure is a nice piece of sable he got on his chin!

FRANKIE

[*Looking off R.*] Well, get a load of Dink!
                    [DINK *enters with* MISS HIGGINS, *a tall
                    girl.*]

MISS HIGGINS

Father!

HIGGINS
              [*Crossing toward them*]

Yes, dear?

MISS HIGGINS

This is Mr. Franklin.

HIGGINS

[*Looking over* DINK's *head*] Where? . . . Oh!
[*Shaking* DINK's *hand warmly*] How do you do, sir?
[*Introducing the group around him*] This is Miss
Honeycutt . . . Mrs. Snow . . . Lieutenant Hodges
. . . and Captain Robbins. . . .
              [DINK *shakes hands all around.*]

MRS. SNOW

[*To* MISS HIGGINS] How did you get out to the club
today?

Carmen Jones

MISS HIGGINS

We took the station wagon. That's all we have now.

HIGGINS

They won't allow us "C" cards any more. We had to put up the Cadillac!

DINK

Hmm! Hmm! I wonder what de poor people are doing!

[*To* MISS HIGGINS] Say, honey, how 'bout you an' me goin' inside an' havin' a beer? I wanna get dis champagne taste outa my mouth!

HIGGINS

But the dancing will start in a few minutes!

MISS HIGGINS

Wouldn't you rather dance to soft music in the moonlight than sit in a bar, drinking beer?

DINK

Frankly . . . no!

[*He exits into the house.*]

HIGGINS

[*To relieve the situation*] Er . . . I think we'd better go down by the swimming pool and start dancing.

[*The* GROUPS *move about preparatory to leaving.* HIGGINS *crosses to* RUM.]

Mr. Daniels! Is that uncouth little man your guest?

RUM

Well, not exactly. He just sorta follered me in. . . .

[CARMEN *enters, top of steps.*]

HIGGINS

As president of this club, I regret to tell you . . .

MYRT

Dere's Carmen!
[MYRT *and* FRANKIE *cross to her.*]

HIGGINS

[*Looking at* CARMEN, *bowled over*] *Who* is that?

RUM

Dat's *another* one of my guests.

HIGGINS

Oh . . . well, that's different!
> [HIGGINS *moves to the group gathered
> around the card table, who ask him about*
> CARMEN, *pointing to her.* RUM *crosses to*
> CARMEN *as she comes down.*]

RUM

Thought you was never goin' to git here!

CARMEN

I had a hard time gittin' away —
[*To* GIRLS] I dressed at your place. I was scared Joe
would foller me dere — but he didn't.

FRANKIE

How you feel your firs' night out?

CARMEN

Like I been born all over agin!

MYRT

Wait'll Husky sees you in dat dicty dress!

RUM

Wait'll he see de bill!

FRANKIE

He won't care. He say to me: "Frankie, you go buy Carmen anything she wants. Only git her to make one date wid me!"

CARMEN

Well, I made de date. Now where *is* he?

RUM

He'll be along soon. I'm sure glad you finally decide to see him.

MYRT

Husky was awful mad dat day we git here an' you got off de train wid Joe.

RUM

Mad! He clipped me so hard dey had to wheel me off de station on a porter's truck!

PRESIDENT

[*Approaching them*] Mr. Daniels, won't you join my party over here?

RUM

Why, certainly —

PRESIDENT

[*Bowing to* CARMEN] I don't believe I've had the pleasure —

RUM

Oh — dis is Mr. Higgins, de president of de club. Dis is Miss Carmen Jones.

Act II. Scene 1

PRESIDENT

How do you do, Miss Jones?

[*He holds out his arm for* CARMEN *to take and leads them all to a table R., proceeding to introduce them to the others. The "Fate" theme introduces the entrance of* JOE *up R. He slides past one of the bushes and comes downstage as unobtrusively as possible. He wears his army trousers, a white shirt with no tie, and a borrowed jacket. He looks pitifully out of place. As the "Fate" theme dies down the conversation can be heard from the group on the opposite side of the stage.*]

GIRL

[*To* CARMEN, FRANKIE, *and* MYRT] Do you girls play gin?

FRANKIE

No ma'am! D'only thing she can do wid cards is tell fortunes.

2ND GIRL

You can? Oh, tell mine.

3RD GIRL

I'm next!

GIRL

Me, too!

[*The* GIRLS *cluster around the card table eagerly.* RUM *spots* JOE, *looks alarmed, and goes to* CARMEN. *He whispers to her and points toward* JOE. *She looks across and sees him.*]

RUM

[*In a low voice*] Carmen, git rid of him soon's you kin.
[RUM *crosses to* PRESIDENT *at group, L., and they exit L., leaving only* MYRT, FRANKIE, *and the* 3 KIBITZERS *around the table.* CARMEN *walks slowly over to* JOE.]

CARMEN

How'd you find dis place?

JOE

Went to where you said de gals lived. Mighty swell flat dey got.

CARMEN

Who tol' you we came here — de servant?

JOE

What's a difference who tol' me? Fac' remains you tried to double-cross me an' I foun' you out!

CARMEN

Look, boy, I don' have to double-cross nobody. Jus' as soon tell de truth. Wanna hear it?
[*Pause. He doesn't.*]

JOE

Lissen, Carmen —

CARMEN

De truth is I cain' stay cooped up in dat back alley no more.

JOE

[*In a fierce whisper*] I *got* to stay dere. You know dat.

CARMEN

You got to, but *I* don't.

JOE

[*Grabbing her arm*] Lissen to me, and lissen good! You is comin' back to dat room wid me — now — you hear?

> [*She neither pulls away nor winces. She returns his look with cool defiance. The force and conviction leave his voice.*]

You's comin' back — wid me.

CARMEN

How'm I goin' *anywheres* wid you — you dressed like you is — an' me dressed up like I am. We'd attrack attenshun, wouldn' we? Ain' good to do dat if you is a deserter!

JOE

[*In a panic, looking about furtively*] Hush your mouth!
[*Lowering his voice*] All we gotta do is git a cab. You grab de nex' one dat drives up to de club. You can pick me up down dere near de gate.
[*Pointing off*] I'll be in de shadder of dat clump o' trees.

CARMEN

> [*Tossing her head toward two commissioned officers who have just entered up L.*]

Dere's some army men. Better not let them see you.

JOE

[*Frightened*] No.
[*He starts, then stops*] Come for me soon's you can. I'll be waitin'.

[*He goes off quickly. She looks after him.*]

CARMEN

[*Cynically, in a low voice*] Okay, boy. You be waitin'.

> [*She walks upstage thoughtfully. Attention is now focused on the card table, where* FRANKIE, MYRT, *and a group of* GIRLS *are engrossed, their eyes glued to the cards.*]

GIRL

Now it's my turn!

OTHER GIRL

> [*Rising and surrendering the chair opposite* FRANKIE]

All right, Susie.

1ST GIRL

[*Sitting*] Can you make my fortune as good as hers?

MYRT

[*Soberly*] No way o' tellin' in advance. De cards don' lie.

FRANKIE

De cards don' lie.

MYRT

[*Pushing a deck toward her subject*] Cut dem.

GROUP OF KIBITZERS and FRANKIE
[*Singing*]

Cut dem!

GIRL

Seven!

FRANKIE

Seven!

MYRT

Da's quite a card!

FRANKIE

Da's quite a card.

GIRL

D'you mean good or bad?

KIBITZERS

Is that good or bad?

MYRT

Quiet, please!

KIBITZERS and FRANKIE

Quiet, please!

> [MYRT *lays the cards out. The others lean over as she concentrates.*]

FRANKIE and MYRT

Will dis gal see
A bright an' happy fewcher?
Or will she be
A good-f'-nuffin' moocher?

MYRT

Come on, you cards, an' tell her true!

GIRL

> [*Anxiety in her voice*]

Come on, you cards, and tell me true!

FRANKIE
An' tell her how she gonna do!

GIRL
An' tell me how I'm going to do!

FRANKIE and MYRT
F'good or bad!
F'high or low!
Come on you cards, an' let 'er know
Whatever way de win' will blow!

> [*About to turn the first card down,*
> FRANKIE *pauses.*]

MYRT
All set?

GIRL
All set!

FRANKIE
F'sho?

THREE GIRLS, MYRT, and FRANKIE
> [*She can't stand much more of this sus-*
> *pense.*]

Let's go!

> [*As they bend over the cards for concen-*
> *trated reading,* CARMEN *picks up another*
> *deck, strolls across to the other side of the*
> *stage, and starts to mix the cards.*]

CARMEN
Le's see what dey say about me.

> [*She cuts the cards. Her eyes freeze with*
> *fright.*]

De nine o' spades!

> [*She mixes up the cards quickly, then cuts them. She cuts the nine of spades!*]

De nine!
Dere he is — de ol' boy!
Plain as kin be!
Death got his han' on me. . . .

> [*She holds the cards; the nine of spades is held apart. She walks downstage. Her worry and fright have given way to the courage innate in her character. Now she sings:*]

It ain' no use to run away f'um dat ol' boy
Ef he is chasin' you.
It's bes' to stan' right up an' look him in de face
When he is facin' you.
Y'gotta be puhpared to go wid dat ol' boy,
No matter what de time.
So I won't fill my pretty eyes wid salty tears —

> [*Her defiance growing*]

Cuz I ain' got de time!
I'm gonna run out ev'ry secon' I got lef'
Before he t'rows me down.
I'm gonna laugh an' sing an' use up all my bref
Before he mows me down!
While I kin fly aroun' I'll do my flyin' high!
I'm gonna keep on livin'
Up to de day I die.

> [*She looks down at the nine of spades.*]

De nine! . . . Hello! — Ol' boy — hello!

> [*The group around the card table, un-*

97

mindful of CARMEN'S *portent of doom, sings.*]

MYRT and FRANKIE

The cards can see
The lady's got a fewcher
And she won't be
A good-for-nothing moocher.

[CARMEN, *pacing up and down, keeps returning to the spot where the nine of spades lies.*]

CARMEN

De nine! . . .

MYRT

De cards'll never lie to you.

CARMEN

Hello!

FRANKIE

De cards'll never lie to you.

CARMEN

De cards don' lie!

MYRT

Dey tell you how you gonna do!

CARMEN

De cards don' lie!
De cards don' lie!

MYRT and FRANKIE

They tell you how you're going to do!
The cards don't lie!

The cards don't lie!
The cards'll tell a fortune
That'll fit a lady like a glove.

FRANKIE
[*Holding up the king of clubs*]

Here's money!

MYRT
[*Holding up jack of hearts*]

An' love!

CARMEN

De cards don' lie!

FRANKIE
[*Cutting again, nine of clubs*]

More money!

MYRT
[*Cutting eight of diamonds*]

More love!

CARMEN

De cards don' lie!
[*The* GIRL, *holding a card in either hand,
gazes at them happily.*]

FRANKIE
[*Pointing to king of clubs in one hand*]

Da's money!

FRANKIE and MYRT
[*Pointing to jack of hearts in other hand*]

Da's love!

ALL

The cards don' lie!

> [CARMEN *exits into house at the conclu-*
> *sion of the "Fortune-Telling" theme. A*
> PHOTOGRAPHER *enters and starts to set*
> *up equipment for flash-bulb pictures.*
> *The* PRESIDENT *enters with* RUM.]

RUM

Here you are, boy. Set 'em up!

PRESIDENT

What is this photographer doing here?

RUM

Little idea I cooked up, Mr. President — dis man is from *Life* Magazine. "Life Goes to a Party at de Meadow Lawn Country Club"! Like de notion?

PRESIDENT

Young man, this is most irregular and unusual.

RUM

You bet it's unusual. It's de smartest fight build-up anybody ever thought of. I'm havin' Husky Miller give a party for Poncho, de panther.

PRESIDENT

Poncho, the panther?

RUM

Champeen of Brazil — feller Husky's gonna fight nex' week —

DINK

[*Appearing in doorway*] Hey, Rum! De dancin' girls you sent for jus' got here. Dey wanna know where dey kin undress.

PRESIDENT

Dancing girls?!

RUM

Just a little entertainment for de Brazilian champeen!

PRESIDENT

As president of the club I forbid it.
Send them all home.

RUM

[*In a panic*] Hey, wait a minute You can't do dat to
me!

PHOTOGRAPHER

And you can't do that to *Life* Magazine!

PRESIDENT

Oh, can't I? Well, as president of this club —

PHOTOGRAPHER

As president of this club are you going to oppose the
good-neighbor policy? Here we have Husky Miller, a
great American athlete, extending the hand of friend-
ship to a Brazilian champion —

RUM

Da's tellin' him!
[*To* PRESIDENT] You hear what de man said?

PRESIDENT

As president of this club —
          [*A* GIRL — *a very pretty and shapely one
          — appears in the doorway.*]

GIRL

Say, boys! Who's goin' to show the girls where they
undress?

Carmen Jones

PRESIDENT

[*Getting a load of her*] As president of this club —
I'll show the girls where they undress.

> [*He exits with the* GIRL. FRANKIE *and*
> MYRT, *who have gone upstage to look off,*
> *now run down to* RUM.]

FRANKIE

Hey, Rum! Here's Husky!

MYRT

Jus' drove up wid Poncho de panther! — an' is dat
boy good-lookin'!

> [*The other* GIRLS *stampede upstage.*]

RUM

Okay! Le's git in a good group to welcome the boys!

PHOTOGRAPHER

[*Shouting*] Tell 'em to cut loose! I want action! These
pictures have got to jump!

> [*Stage-managed by* RUM, *the group on*
> *stage starts to sing out their welcome.*]

GIRLS and MEN

Poncho, de panther from Brazil!
What a man!
A man would be a fool to fool wid
Poncho, de punchin' cavalero,
De champ o' Rio de Janeiro!

> [*On a repeat refrain,* HUSKY *and* PONCHO
> *enter, both in evening dress. They pose*
> *and the flash-bulbs get busy*]

MEN

[*As* RUM *holds up* HUSKY'S *hand*]

He's from de north —

GIRLS

An' his name is Husky Miller!

MEN

[*As* RUM *holds up* PONCHO'S *hand*]

He's from de south —

GIRLS

He's a Latin killer-diller!

[*Now* RUM *poses them in a handshake.*]

ALL

Dere shakin' han's,
An' dey wan' de worl' to know
Dere shakin' han's
'Cross de Gulf o' Mexico!

[HUSKY *leads the final refrain, his hand
on* PONCHO'S *shoulder.*]

HUSKY and ALL

Poncho, you panther from Brazil!
Welcome here!
Come here, an' have yourself a party.
Poncho, yore welcome in Chicago,
You can unpack your brush an' comb,
Make yourself at home!
Come an' make Chicago your home!

[*They have led him to a chair and seated
him. Now* HUSKY *sits beside him. The
coda which follows this singing refrain is*

utilized to bring the DANCERS *on, and now
the stage is left to the* DANCERS *who per-
form a ballet in honor of the distinguished
visitor. It is a mixture of Spanish and
Harlem. After the dance there is a gen-
eral exit into the house, perhaps reprising
the refrain used for their entrance.*
HUSKY *and* RUM *are the last to go off.*
HUSKY *lingers and detains* RUM *so that
he can get some information about the
subject nearest his heart.*]

HUSKY

Hey, Rum! I thought you said you was goin' to git
Carmen here tonight.

RUM

I *did* git her here. She's right inside.

HUSKY

She is? Well, what're we waitin' for?
[*He starts for the clubhouse with* RUM.
Now BULLET HEAD, *brawny, athletic man
as big as* HUSKY, *runs on and calls in a
hoarse whisper:*]

BULLET HEAD

Husky!
[HUSKY *and* RUM *turn.*]

RUM

What you doin' here, Bullet Head? Husky don' need
no sparrin' partner tonight.

BULLET HEAD

I wouldna come, but she said it was a matter of life
an' death.

HUSKY

Who said?

BULLET HEAD

Dis girl.

RUM

What girl?

> [BULLET HEAD *looks behind him, but she
> is not there. She is hanging back timidly
> near the corner of the house. He spots
> her.*]

BULLET HEAD

Hey, come outa dere an' show yourself.

> [*She comes down slowly, shy and fright-
> ened. It is* CINDY LOU.]

She come to de trainin' quarters jus' as you was
leavin' —

RUM

[*Suspiciously*] Do you know who she is, Husky?

HUSKY

Never see her before in my life.

BULLET HEAD

[*Defending himself*] She said it was a matter of life
an' death. Made me ride her over on my motorcycle.

> [*The 3* MEN *look at* CINDY. *It takes a few
> seconds of silence for her to force enough
> courage to speak.*]

CINDY

I jus' had to see you, Mr. Miller. . . .

HUSKY

Where you come from?

CINDY

A long ways away. Sat up all night on de train. Got into Chicago dis afternoon. . . . Come straight to you.

HUSKY

[*Flattered, he grins at the other men. They wink back.*]

An' you do all dis jus' cuz you wanted to see Husky Miller?

CINDY

N-no, not ex*ackly*. I wanna see a feller name Joe.
[HUSKY *is deflated.*]
I thought mebbe you could tell me where he is at. — I know you all come up north on de same train —

HUSKY

[*Scratching his head*] Honey, you talkin' all over your mouth, but de words don' connec'!

CINDY

[*Continuing, perseveringly*] I come down to meet Joe dat night cuz I knowed he was gettin' outa de guard-house — an' I had some candy an' cakes for him. Well, de bus stop is right near de railroad station an' jus' as I got dere, I saw him gittin' on de train — wid dat woman. My heart freeze up inside me!

RUM

I think she talkin' 'bout dat feller Carmen bring up here.

CINDY

Da's right, Carmen! She de one take my Joe!

RUM

I see! You Joe's ol' girl frien', dat it?

> [CINDY *nods and turns away. Nudging* HUSKY, *and whispering*]

Dis a good break for you. Maybe we git rid of him dis-a-way.

HUSKY

[*Out of the side of his mouth, to* RUM] Da's what I was thinkin'.

[*He turns to* CINDY] You jus' wait here, sweetie, an' we'll go ask Carmen where Joe is at —

CINDY

Carmen! She here?

RUM

Sure — she can tell you all right. Bullet Head, you wait in de parkin' lot till we see if we need you.

> [BULLET HEAD *exits.* RUM *and* HUSKY *start to exit, then* HUSKY *turns back.*]

HUSKY

Say, li'l gal, I wan' you to 'splain sumpin' to me. Dis Joe, he ain' a very good-lookin' feller as I remember.

CINDY

No, not 'specially —

HUSKY

But Carmen brung him up to Chicago —
[*Thinking it over*] Den *you* chase him all away· up
here. Say! What's he got?

CINDY

[*Humbly*] I don' know, Mr. Miller.

HUSKY

He was awful mean to you, wasn''he?

CINDY

I guess *so*.

HUSKY

Den why you run af'er him?
              [*Pause.*]

CINDY

Seem like I love him, I guess.

HUSKY

But why?

CINDY

I don't know, Mr. Miller.

HUSKY

Women is de craziest people I ever met!
              [*He exits with* RUM. *His comment starts
              a train of thought in* CINDY's *mind.*]

CINDY

How kin I love a man when I know he don' wan' me?
He ain' been good. He ain' been kind.
He gimme up for a ol' roadside woman —
But I cain' drive him from my mind!

[She closes her eyes and starts to remember.]

My Joe,
He wuz always my Joe.
Dere wuz no one but me —
Joe said dere never could be.
We wuz in love
An' I reckon we showed it.
F'um de way people talked,
Reckon ev'ryone knowed it.
Kids on de street where we'd go
Use ter yell at us:
"Cindy Lou belongs to Joe!"
Lawd! O Lawd, y'know dat dat wuz true,
An' Joey belonged to Cindy Lou.

[She glances around at her unfamiliar surroundings and is suddenly frightened.]

I is skeered.
O Lawd! I is skeered!
I'se like a leaf dat los' her tree.
I'se alone.
O Lawd! I'se alone!
He got hisse'f anudder woman.
Now she got his arms all aroun' her —

[She covers her eyes with her hands.]

No, Lawd! I cain' believe it's so.
No! No! Don' yer let her keep my Joe.
Make him t'row her back where he foun' her!

[Desperation in her voice as she shouts his name.]

Joe! Y'said dat both your arms wuz mine —
Remember? Y'said your arms wuz mine.

I'se yo' gal,
I wuz always yo' gal
Dere wuz no one but me,
You said dere never could be.
We wuz in love
An' I reckon we showed it.
F'um de way people talked,
Reckon ev'ryone knowed it.
Kids on de street where we'd go
Useter yell at us:
"Cindy Lou belongs to Joe!"
Lawd! O Lawd, look down
An' try to see
How you kin make Joe come home to me.

           [*Looking up in fervent prayer*]

O Lawd look down.
Lead my Joe
Off de road
Where he strayin'.
Oh, tell my man
Where to go—
O Lawd, I'se callin' on you!

           [*She walks upstage and sinks down on a
chair.* JOE *enters U.R. not seeing* CINDY.
*He crosses toward the clubhouse. Hesi-
tating for an instant at C., he starts, with
sudden decision, for the house.* CINDY
calls on him.]

Joe!

Act II. Scene 1

[JOE *turns slowly. Music is played beneath the following scene.* JOE *blinks, looking at* CINDY *as if he can't believe she's there.*]

Didn' 'spec to fin' you so quick. Seem like de Lawd jus' guided me to you.

JOE

What you doin' here, Cindy?

CINDY

I come to git you back home. I know dey lookin' for you. But I figger we could sneak through our town in de night an' I'd git you into my house an' keep you dere. I'd take good keer o' you, Joe —

[*Pause.* CARMEN'S *laugh is heard approaching.*]

JOE

[*In a dull, flat voice*] I ain' no good to you, Cindy. Go on home!

HUSKY

[*Entering with* CARMEN] Dere she is —
[*He stops short.*] Oh — She foun' him already. How'd *he* git here?

JOE

[*Looking across at* CARMEN *and* HUSKY, *bitter sarcasm in his voice*] Well, don' dey make a good-lookin' couple!

CARMEN

Thought you was goin' to wait down dere under de trees.

111

JOE

Sure you did! You thought I was goin' to wait all
night —

HUSKY

What's dis jerk talkin' 'bout, Carmen?

JOE

You be keerful what you call me, mister!

HUSKY

Who I be keerful of?

CARMEN

Take it easy, Joe. You don' wanna git in no fight wid
Husky.

HUSKY

[*Indicating* CINDY] Why'n't you go 'way wid dis sweet
li'l gal? She come two thousan' miles to see you.

JOE

[*Wheeling on him savagely*] Why don' you shut dat
big mouth o' yours?
[*Shouting at* CARMEN] Dis yore new man, ain't he?
Sure! He's a big strappin' boy. Maybe give you a better time den me. . . . 'Side dat he's a big shot! Maybe
you git yore pitcher in de paper 'longside him — so
ev'ybody c'n know who is Husky Miller's lates'
woman —

> [*He grabs* CARMEN *roughly, but* HUSKY
> *sails in, yanks him away, and hurls him
> across the stage.* CINDY *runs over to him.*]

CINDY

Joe, come away —

JOE

[*Slinging her off*] Lea' me alone —
[*He faces* HUSKY, *his voice quavering desperately.*] I
swore if dis was de way it was, I'd never let you git
her — never let you nor no man take her away from
me.

HUSKY

How you goin' to stop me?

JOE

I'll show you —
> [*He whips out a pocket-knife and un-
> clasps it quickly.*]

I'll show you how!
> [*He rushes at* HUSKY. CINDY *shrieks.*
> HUSKY *grabs the wrist that holds the knife.*
> *They struggle.* RUM *and* DINK *run on, and*
> *mix in. They disarm* JOE *and hold back*
> HUSKY. *The* CLUB PRESIDENT *comes on.*
> FRANKIE *and* MYRT *stand in the door-*
> *way.*]

HUSKY

Git away from me, Rum. I'm goin' to kill dat li'l rat
if it's de las' thing I do!

RUM

[*Holding him*] Dat would be de las' thing you'd do.
Now calm down!

DINK

C'mon, Husky! Cool off an' ack like folks.

CLUB PRESIDENT

[*Pointing to* JOE] Who is this man?

DINK

He come on de groun's an' attack Husky. It's a case o' salt an' battery.

MYR'T

Shall I phone the police?

RUM

No, don' do dat. We don' wan' dis in de paper!

CLUB PRESIDENT

[*Angrily*] *We* don't want it in the paper either.

RUM

[*To* PRESIDENT] You go inside an' keep people from comin' out. I'll git rid of dis feller.
[*To* HUSKY] You go in, too, Husky.

HUSKY

I'd jus' like one crack —

DINK

C'mon, Husky. Save your knuckles for de *big* fight nex' week. Save 'em for Poncho.

> [DINK *leads him off. The* CLUB PRESI-
> DENT *exits, too.*]

CARMEN

[*To* JOE] Better go 'way wid dis gal like she wan's you to.

RUM

'Bout time you lef' town anyways. De army'll be af'er you hot an' heavy —

JOE

Let 'em come.

RUM

You gotta look out for yourself, man.

CINDY

It ain' jus' yourself, Joe, I come up 'counta somebody else.

JOE

[*Turning slowly*] What you mean, Cindy?

CINDY

I come for some one else. . . .
                    [*Singing*]
Your Maw is lonesome an' worried cuz you stay away
    so long —
She cain' sleep in de night now an' she don' feel none
    too strong.
So she tol' me to come an' find you
An' to say she is sick an' blue.
She tol' me to remind you
Dat you's all she got —
All she got in de world is you!

CARMEN

You oughta go an' see your Maw,
You better go an' see your Maw —

JOE

You would like dat I reckon!

CARMEN

[*Urging him toward* CINDY]

Go wid de lady now!

JOE

You would like dat, I reckon!
You would like to git me away.

115

Dat'd leave you free to play —
No! No you don't!
                    [*With intense determination*]
Y'know you are tied to me,
An' y'know you'll never git away.
Yore de shore an' I'm de sea,
By my side yore tied to stay!
Where you go I'm goin' too,
An' when you die I'm gonna die wid you!

          FRANKIE, MYRT, and RUM
Leave de gal an' go away
She got a life of her own,
Leave de gal an' go away.
Go away! Leave her alone!

                    CINDY
Oh, lissen, Joe, lemme say
A word for yore ear alone
Cuz I gotta say what I come to say,
An' it must be known!

                    JOE
Lemme be!

                    CINDY
Don't turn from me — Joe, lissen to me — Dr.
Kirby —
                    [JOE *turns sharply*.]
Dr. Kirby, he say —

                    JOE
[*Grabbing* CINDY *by the shoulders*] Sumpin' de matter
wid my Maw?

116

CINDY

You gotta come home right away if you wanna see her
before — before —

JOE

She gonna die?

> [CINDY *lowers her eyes.* MYRT, FRANKIE,
> RUM, *and* DINK *slowly move upstage.*
> JOE's *hands slowly drop from* CINDY's
> *shoulders. He turns slowly and looks at*
> CARMEN.]

CINDY

Dr. Kirby give me de money to come an' fetch you.
He knows what it'd mean to your Maw to see you jus'
once.

> [*He continues to stare at* CARMEN.]

You comin', Joe?

JOE

[*Not taking his eyes from* CARMEN] Look what kind
o' man I am, now! My Maw is dyin' an' I'm standin'
here wond'rin' how I can leave dat woman — even for
a little while.

CARMEN

[*Ironically*] Why for a *little* while?

CINDY

You comin', Joe?

CARMEN

You goin', Joe?

> [JOE *looks at* CINDY *then turns back to*
> CARMEN.]

JOE

Yes. I'm goin' — but I'll be back. Don' worry 'bout dat, Carmen, I'll be back.

CARMEN

Maybe I won' be here no more.

JOE

I'll foller you — no matter where you go.

CARMEN

Won' do no good. Once you get away from me, be better if you *stay* away.

JOE

[*As if it were his heart rising to his throat to cry out its protest*]

No!. . . .

[*He grabs* CARMEN *and holds her with a grip of iron as he sings:*]

No!
Where I go you go wid me,
An' you know dat's de way it's gotta be,
Down to hell or up to heav'n —
Down rivers an' 'cross de sea —
Where you go I'm goin' too,
An' when you die I'm gonna die wid you!

[CINDY *takes his hand, but he throws it off and starts away. He stops for one more look at* CARMEN, *then exits, followed by* CINDY, *to the "Doom" theme.* MYRT, FRANKIE, DINK, *and* RUM *look after them. The refrain of "Stan' Up an' Fight" is heard sung by* HUSKY *off in the house.*]

118

Act II. Scene 1

CARMEN *turns her eyes from the direction in which* JOE *made his exit and looks toward the clubhouse. She then walks slowly toward the house. One more look at* JOE'S *direction, a shrug, a smile, then she turns and walks up to join her new man, as the* CURTAIN FALLS.]

ACT II.   Scene 2

Outside a baseball park. The night of the big fight. One week later.

At rise: A typical fight crowd, milling about the stage. Boys selling programs, fans, soft drinks, popcorn, etc. Children chasing each other, getting into fights, and being threatened by park policemen; pickpockets, tarts, and respectable family parties. . . .

BASSES
Git a program for de big fight!

BASSES and TENORS
Git yer program for de big fight!

ALL
Git a weenie on a roll, a
Glass of ice-col' Coca-Cola!

> [*A group of* HIGH-SCHOOL GIRLS *enter, with their boy friends.*]

HIGH-SCHOOL GIRLS
Oh, baby! What a dreamy night!
Gonna see Husky Miller fight!
What it cost to come to de fight?

BOYS
Four bucks!

GIRLS
Four bucks!

BOYS
Da's what dey rolled me!

MEN

[*Referring to this group*] I bet dem little debutants
Got dere name on dere underpants!

OTHER MEN

Some o' dem don' wear underpants!

OLD MAN WITH EAR-TRUMPET

What's dat?

MEN

[*Shouting in his ear*] Dat's what a feller told me!

TENORS

Git a cushion for de lady!
Git a cushion for de lady!
She will see more of de fight,
She won' be sore when de fight's over!

> [*A flashily dressed gambler enters, with his henchmen and 3 or 4 sportin' gals. The following lines are spoken.*]

SLAPPY

[*Shouting*] Dat's Balloon-Cheeks Buckley, de big gambler!

> [SLAPPY, *a down-and-out boxer in the "punchy" stage, accosts the gambler.*]

SLAPPY

Hi, Balloon Cheeks! Could you loan me ten bucks?

BALLOON CHEEKS

[*Fishing in his pocket and doling it out*] Here y'are, Slappy!

> [*Now 2 fan-selling* BOYS *come forward.*]

TENORS and SOPRANOS

Who wants to buy a pretty fan?

Got a dime for a pretty fan?

Gittin' pow'ful hot in de stan'!

[GIRLS *fan themselves and the handles break right off!*]

MEN

What's dat?

GIRLS

Dat's what a feller sold me!

[PONCHO, *the Panther, enters with a snappily dressed group of Brazilians. They positively glitter as they cross the stage.*]

MAN

Here comes de Panther!

MAN

Hi, Poncho!

GIRL

Is he sump'n!

MAN

Here comes de Panther.

BOY

Good luck, Poncho!

GIRL

You need it, Poncho!

MAN

Hi, Poncho!

122

ALL

Wait'll Husky Miller hits him!
Wait'll Husky Miller hits him!
He'll knock dat big Rhumba man
Clear back to Rio de Jan-ei-ro!

> [*One of the Panther's party resents this
> and gets into a fracas with a supporter of
> HUSKY. The PARK POLICE separate them.
> PONCHO and his friends exit.*]

POLICE

Move along, dere!
Move along, dere!
Move along, dere!
Git on your way!

> [*Some* KIDS *run on excitedly. The* KIDS
> *jump up and down and shout:*]

KIDS

He's comin'! He's comin'! He's comin'!

GIRL

Who's comin'?

KID

I seed him!

GIRL

Who'd you see?

MAN

[*Getting his breath*] Husky Miller!

GIRL

Husky Miller!

123

MAN

[*Pointing over audience toward the back*] See dat open taxi? He's in it!

GIRL

Crowd's so thick I cain' see nothin'!

2ND GIRL

I see him! He's standin' up in de taxi! Signin' autographs!

[*Balance of this episode will be sung.*]

CHILDREN

[SOPRANOS *sing this. The* CHILDREN *jump up and down and climb on people's backs to suit the words with action.*]

Lemme see! Lemme see!
I wanna see Husky!

ALL

Husky! Husky!

BASSES

Dere he is!

TENORS

Dere he is!

SOPRANOS

Dere he is!

SOPRANOS and TENORS

De kid himself!
Well, looka dat Husky!

[*In a transport of joy and passionate homage everybody sings now.*]

124

ALL

Dat's our man, de man wid de wallop,
Hotter dan a firecracker!
When he land dat ol' belly-whacker —
Kayo! Kayo! Kayo!
Atta boy, Husky, make wid de wallop!
Win dat dough an' den you can doll up,
Wid a di'mon big as a scallop!
Atta boy!
  Atta boy!
    Atta boy!

> [*Now they dance to let off steam. . . .*
> *After the dance the small fry take the*
> *foreground. The* BOYS *flex their biceps*
> *and the* GIRLS *feel them.*]

KIDS
[*Again supported by* SOPRANOS]

When I'm big an' strong as Husky
I'll go home an' lick my Pa!
I will make a million dollars
An' I'll give it all to Ma!

POLICE
[*Shooing the* KIDS *away*]

Move on! Move on! Move on! Move on!

ALL

Cheese it, kids, here come de cops!

POLICE

Move on! Move on! Move on! Move on!

KIDS
[*Behind the backs of the* POLICE]

Yah!

POLICE
Move on! Move on! Move on! Move on!

ALL
[*Derisively*]

Yah! Yah! Yah! Yah! Yah! Yah! Yah! Yah!
[*The* POLICE *gone,* 4 BOYS *start to dance.
At the end of this dancing interlude,*
DANCING GIRLS *line up downstage and
primp to receive* HUSKY.]

MEN
Git a load of all dem tomayters!
Linin' up so dey can ketch his eye!
[*To* GIRLS]
No hope! No soap!
He's got a woman —
Bait yer hook fer fish you can fry!
[*They come forward. The* GIRLS *shun
them.*]

GIRLS
[*Sung by the* SINGERS, *acted by the*
DANCERS]

Go 'way! Go 'way f'um me, go 'way!
I gotta have a man wid shoulders!
Go 'way, go 'way, go 'way!
Give me de man de people come to see —
You's only ticket-holders!

MEN

Okay! Okay!

KIDS

Go 'way!

GIRLS

When he comes by
I'm gonna try!
When he comes by
I'm gonna try!

MEN

Go fish fer fish
Dat you can fry!
> [*The* CHILDREN *have discovered something and start to jump up and down excitedly.*]

SOPRANOS

Dere jus' gittin' outa de taxi!
Dere jus' gittin' outa de taxi!

TENORS

Dere headin' right dis way!

SOPRANOS

Dere headin' right dis way!

BASSES

Dere headin' right dis way!

SOPRANOS

He's got a gal!
He's de only man I would die for —
But, of course, he *would* have a gal!

127

BASSES

[*Organizing the crowd to greet the approaching* HUSKY]

Come on, now!

SOPRANOS

Come on, now!

TENORS

Togedder!

SOPRANOS

Togedder!

> [HUSKY *enters with* CARMEN, *both look-
> ing resplendent. He beams grandly at the
> crowd and she beams proudly at him.*
> RUM, DINK, MYRT, *and* FRANKIE *follow on
> later.*]

Husky Miller!

> [*And the* TENORS *and* BASSES, *and* ALL,
> *repeat his name in an enthusiastic and
> climactic greeting. Then they sing their
> lungs out in frank adulation:*]

ALL

Husky Miller!
Stan' up an' fight until you hear de bell,

> [HUSKY *and* CARMEN *enter.*]

Stan' toe to toe,
Trade blow for blow!
Keep punchin' till you make yer punches tell,
Show dat crowd whatcher know!

> [RUM, FRANKIE, DINK, *and* MYRT *enter.*]

Until you hear dat bell,

Dat final bell,
Stan' up an —

> [*They mill around him and dance and
> shout while the* POLICE *try to make a lane
> for him to cross the stage.*]

ALL

Dat's our man, de man wid de wallop,
Hotter dan a firecracker!
When y' lan' dat ol' belly-whacker —
Kayo! Kayo! Kayo!
Atta boy, Husky, make wid de wallop!
Win dat dough an' den you can doll up,
Wid a di'mon big as a scallop —

SOPRANOS

Atta baby!

BASSES

Atta baby!

TENORS

Atta baby!

ALL

Hey!
Husky Miller!
Husky Miller!

BASSES

Husky —

TENORS and SOPRANOS

Miller!

BASSES

Husky —

TENORS and SOPRANOS

Miller!

BASSES

Husky —

TENORS and SOPRANOS

Husky —

ALL

Miller!

[*This thing has gone far enough now. An ovation is an ovation, but* HUSKY *has a big fight tonight, so* RUM *and* DINK, *with the help of the* POLICE, *strong-arm the crowd out of the way and get* HUSKY *off. The cheering continues till he's out of sight. He blows a kiss back at* CARMEN *over the heads of the crowd before he goes. The* CROWD *breaks into groups — and follow* HUSKY *off.* CARMEN, *downstage, is approached by* FRANKIE *and* MYRT, *who have been looking off stage at something that has brought worry to their faces.*]

FRANKIE

[*Nudging* CARMEN] Hey, look! Look over dere! Do you see what I see?

CARMEN

Which way you mean? Over where?

MYRT

He looks mean.

CARMEN

Who's dat?

MYRT

Joe! Your ol' friend — over dere by de lamp-post.
Y'see him?

CARMEN

[*Peering past her shoulder*] Yep. Dat's his nibs!

MYRT

Thought he went home.

CARMEN

[*Continuing to look off*] He did. But he said he'd come
back.
[*Fatalistically*] I knowed he would, too!

FRANKIE

[*Taking* CARMEN'S *arm*] Come away!

CARMEN

Whose afraid of him? What can he do to me?
Let him come. Git it over wid now!

MYRT

He's nuts! Suppose he kills you?

CARMEN

Ain't gonna run away — from him or no one!

FRANKIE

Child, you's whacky!
[CARMEN *waves them aside and they with-
draw to the left side, hesitantly, leaving
her to stand her ground alone and face
JOE. He enters R. slowly. He is thin, hag-
gard, unshaven, and dirty. His eyes have
the wild look of an over-tired, over-har-*

*assed man. The theme of "Dat's our
man" hurries the rest of the* CROWD *off
stage, rushing to their seats to see the
fight. As the music quiets down,* MYRT
and FRANKIE *down L. speak quickly and
quietly:*]

MYRT
D'army police are still lookin' for him, ain' dey?

FRANKIE
I don' like to snitch on nobody — but maybe we better —

> [*They exit.* JOE *now walks closer to* CAR-
> MEN. *He is frightening to look upon, but
> she doesn't back away an inch*]

CARMEN
You didn' stay home long —

JOE
My Maw was dead when I got dere.

CARMEN
Myrt an' Frankie jus' tell me you was headin' my way.
Dey say I better scram. Dey say y' might git mean an'
maybe try an' kill me.
[*Looking him straight in the eye*] You got your chance.
Kill me now! Here I am!

JOE
But all I want to do is love you like I useter,
To hol' your han' in my han'
An' feel your heart nex' to my heart.
Cain' we begin again?

Couldn' we start all over?
Couldn' we begin again?

CARMEN

If you wanna start a fire where a fire was before,
De coal you burn mus' be *new* coal!
Our flame is out — cold as de snow!
We had oursel's some fun — didn' we?
          [*He comes toward her. She turns away.*]
An' now it's done!

JOE

But where can I put my mem'ries?
Dey got no sea to drown in —
De little things
Dat useter make us laugh
When we was clownin',
An' all de things we'd say or do
Are all part of me an' you —

CARMEN

Joe, you is makin' it tough now,
Fer y'self, de same as fer me.
          [*Her nerves tightening*]
Joe! Ain' you heard me say enough, now?
          [*Shrieking*]
No! No! NO! —
What useter be ain' no mo'!

JOE	CARMEN
But where kin y'put your mem'ries?	Oh, why mus' you keep on poun'in',
Dey got no sea to drown in —	Poun'in' out de same ol' tune?

De little t'ings dat use ter
   make us laugh
When we was clownin'
An' all de things we'd say
   or do
Are all part of me and
   you!
Do you fergit
How I use ter love you?
No one but Joe
Ever loved y'so good.
Le's go away an' begin
   our life all over,
Carmen all alone wid Joe.

Why should I say
I love yer,
When I don' no mo'?
No, I don' no mo'!
Don' be dat way!
Give up
   what you don' own no
      mo'!

Don' y't'ink dere's a
   chance?
Only say dat y'do!

CARMEN

No . . . dat wouldn't be true!

> [*She becomes impatient and suddenly
> and fiercely rebellious at all this weak
> and dishonest temporizing.*

Ain' gonna lie! Ain' gonna lie!
I look at life straight in de eye!

> [*Off stage, in the stadium,* HUSKY'S AD-
> MIRERS *can be heard singing:* "*Dat's our
> man!*"]

CHORUS

Dat's our man, de man wid de wallop,
Hotter dan a firecracker!

When he lands dat ol' belly-whacker —
Kayo! Kayo! Kayo!
Atta boy, Husky.
Make wid de wallop!
Win dat dough an' den you can doll up,
Wid a dimon' big as a scallop!
Kayo! Kayo! Kayo!
Let's go!

> [CARMEN *involuntarily moves toward the
> sound. A proud smile comes into her face.*
> JOE *notices this and it is a bitter pill. As
> the refrain finishes she starts to go.* JOE
> *gets in front of her. The music in the
> orchestra becomes ominously dramatic
> under the following speeches:*]

JOE

Where you goin'?

CARMEN

Up to de gran' stan'. Got a seat in a box!

JOE

[*Grabbing her wrist*] You ain' goin' to no seat in no
box! You comin' wid me — you comin' wid me or
you ain' goin' no place.

CARMEN

[*Struggling to free herself*] Lemme go! Don' you see
dis won' do you no good?

> [*Singing, softly at first, then finishing the
> phrase* forte]

I love him!
Why cain' you get dat through yer head?

> [*Pointing toward the stadium*]

He is de man I want —
>   [*Rising to a defiant screech*]
An' I love him!
>   [*Again the* CROWD *is heard singing in the
>   stadium.*]

CHORUS

Dat's our man.
De man wid de wallop!
Hotter dan a firecracker!
When he lands dat ol' belly-whacker —
Kayo! Kayo! Kayo!
Atta boy, Husky.
Make wid de wallop!
Win dat dough!
Come on, let 'er go!
>   [JOE *continues to hold* CARMEN'S *wrist,
>   a dull, cold look in his eye. She tries to
>   outstare him but something makes her
>   look away this time. She senses that this
>   is it. This is her hour of doom. She knows
>   he will kill her, even before he knows it
>   himself. At the end of the singing the
>   "Fate" theme is played and comes in
>   again and again with terrifying, insistent
>   repetition, in between all the following
>   speeches:*]

JOE

I ain' goin' to let you go!
>   [*The theme*]
Ain' goin' to have no man laughin' at me while you
rollin' in his arms!

CARMEN

Lemme go!
>   [*Theme*]

JOE

You come wid me or — or I'll kill you!

CARMEN

Kill me, den! Kill me now or let me go!
>   [*Theme*]

JOE

For de las' time —

CARMEN

For de las' time —
>   [*She yanks a ring off her finger.*]

Here's dat ten-cent-store ring you give me —
>   [*She throws it away from her.*]

Da's de end of you!
>   [*The sky comes tumbling down over
>   JOE's head and there is no more world.*]

JOE

You bitch! You gimme love — den you kill it right in
front of my eyes! Y'ain' never goin' to do dat to no
man again!
>   [*She starts to go. He grabs her and holds
>   her with a grip of iron. With his free hand
>   he draws a knife from his pocket. She
>   doesn't move now. Her eyes stay on the
>   knife, fascinated with fright. He twists
>   her arm till she drops to her knees up-
>   stage of JOE, so that she is partly covered
>   by him. The CROWD in the stadium starts*]

*to sing: "Stan' up an' fight." JOE raises
his knife high and strikes down hard. His
back is to the audience and CARMEN is upstage of him so that the actual hit of the
knife can't be seen. She sinks to the
ground. JOE stands, transfixed, staring
down at the limp body. Behind a scrim
the stage lights up revealing the stadium,
the ring under its hard white light, and
the CROWD surrounding it, roaring their
song of triumph. PONCHO and HUSKY are
in a clinch. After a brief struggle HUSKY
lands on him and PONCHO is on the can-
vas. HUSKY stands in his corner and the
referee is counting. The tableau of CAR-
MEN and JOE downstage is now seen only
in the light reflected from the ring upstage. During this action the CROWD
sings:]*

ALL

Stan' up an' fight until you hear de bell.
Stan' toe to toe,
Trade blow for blow!
Keep punchin' till you
Make yer punches tell.
Show dat crowd
What you know!
Until you hear dat bell,
Dat final bell,
Jus' fight
Like hell!

Act II.   Scene 2

[*The* REFEREE *holds up* HUSKY'S *hand.
The wildly singing, cheering* CROWD,
HUSKY *and the* REFEREE, *all suddenly
freeze into a still picture — and hold it.
The lights dim on this background as*
CARMEN *and* JOE *downstage become
lighted more distinctly.*

JOE
[*On his knees*]
String me high on a tree
So dat I soon will be
Wid my darlin', my baby —
    [*His voice breaking*]
My Carmen!
    [*He throws himself across her body and
embraces her.*]

This book is composed on the Linotype in Bodoni, so called after Giambattista Bodoni (1740–1813), son of a printer of Piedmont. After gaining experience and fame as superintendent of the Press of the Propaganda in Rome, Bodoni became in 1766 the head of the ducal printing house at Parma, which he soon made the foremost of its kind in Europe. His Manuale Tipografico, completed by his widow in 1818, contains 279 pages of specimens of types, including alphabets of about thirty foreign languages. His editions of Greek, Latin, Italian, and French classics, especially his Homer, are celebrated for their typography. In type-designing he was an innovator, making his new faces rounder, wider, and lighter, with greater openness and delicacy. His types were rather too rigidly perfect in detail, the thick lines contrasting sharply with the thin wiry lines. It was this feature, doubtless, that caused William Morris's condemnation of the Bodoni types as "swelteringly hideous." Bodoni Book, as reproduced by the Linotype Company, is a modern version based, not upon any one of Bodoni's fonts, but upon a composite conception of the Bodoni manner, designed to avoid the details stigmatized as bad by typographical experts and to secure the pleasing and effective results of which the Bodoni types are capable.

This book was composed, printed, and bound by THE PLIMPTON PRESS, *Norwood, Mass · The typographic scheme and binding design are by* W. A. DWIGGINS.